PRAISE FOR
THE SENIOR

This is one of the best sports stories I have ever seen. An all-timer!

— JIM ROME,
host of *Jim Rome is Burning*

Almost everyone has some regrets in life and almost everyone has experienced the death of a dream. Rare are the opportunities we get for a "do over." *The Senior* is a great read about a man who was faced with an opportunity for a "do over" nearly 40 years later in life and had the courage to do it. Mike Flynt's story is one of the most inspirational you will ever read. Everyone who picks up this book is going to be encouraged through the journey of one man who placed his faith in God and had the courage to face his past. It is a joy to be Mike's friend and pastor.

— RICK WHITE,
Senior Pastor, The People's Church,
Franklin, TN

Mike worked in our strength training program many years ago and eventually fulfilled a lifelong dream to finish off his playing career on the right side of the ledger. To do so at a rather advanced age is remarkable. I think that readers will find the story to be fascinating.

— TOM OSBORNE,
former Head Football Coach,
University of Nebraska,
Author of *Faith in the Game*

The Mike Flynt story is absolutely awesome! You will read this book in one sitting, just like I did. I loved it!

— PAT WILLIAMS,
Senior Vice President,
Orlando Magic,
Author of *The Pursuit*

THE SENIOR

THE SENIOR

MIKE FLYNT

AND

DON YAEGER

THOMAS NELSON
Since 1798

NASHVILLE DALLAS MEXICO CITY RIO DE JANEIRO BEIJING

Published in Nashville, Tennessee, by Thomas Nelson. Thomas Nelson is a registered trademark of Thomas Nelson, Inc.

Published in association with the literary agency of Mark Sweeney & Associates, Bonita Springs, Florida 34135

Thomas Nelson, Inc., titles may be purchased in bulk for educational, business, fund-raising, or sales promotional use. For information, please e-mail SpecialMarkets@ThomasNelson.com.

Scripture quotations are taken from the King James Version. Public domain.

Library of Congress Cataloging-in-Publication Data

Flynt, Mike.
    The senior : my amazing year as a 59-year-old college football linebacker / by Mike Flynt.
      p. cm.
    ISBN 978-0-8499-2063-9 (hardcover)
    1. Flynt, Mike. 2. Football players—United States—Biography. 3. Linebackers (Football)—United States—Biography. 4. Older men—United States—Biography. I. Title.
GV939.F59A3 2008
796.332092—dc22
[B]
                                                            2008023044

Printed in the United States of America

08 09 10 11 12 QW 5 4 3 2 1

To Eileen:

My time in this world is measured before and after Eileen, the love of my life who has always believed in me. Thank you for encouraging me to dream and then helping to make my dreams come true. I love you with all my heart.

To my Dad:

For all the things he taught me, right or wrong, no father ever loved a son more than my dad loved me.

CONTENTS

FOREWORD BY LEBRON JAMES

When I grab a book or magazine in search of a little mental escape, I am always looking for a good story. I want to read about others who have overcome obstacles, about people who have shown that limits are something you place on yourself. I read to be inspired. That's what drew me to the story of a fifty-nine-year-old man trying to make a college football team in South Texas. As soon as I read that story in a magazine, I wanted to know more about him and why he was taking the risk. The more I learned about Mike Flynt, the more I wanted to learn. The more of the story I knew, the more I wanted to help him tell it.

When I started my management company in 2005 with childhood friends Richard Paul, Maverick Carter, and Randy Mims, I knew exactly what I wanted to do. I wanted our approach to be seen as visionary in the business world and totally different than any other management company out there. I had complete confidence in my plan, but I knew I needed to surround myself with people who shared my values, people of character who inspire and help others to be better. That is why Mike Flynt's story is one that I chose to highlight as the first of many we hope to see associated with our company.

Mike never gave up his dream, even at age fifty-nine. He never allowed anyone to take away that dream, no matter how old he was or what he went through, and that's why I was so inspired by his determination. I first met Mike at one of my Cleveland Cavaliers' home games in November 2007. Mike had been talking with Maverick Carter, CEO of our management company, LRMR Innovative Marketing & Branding, and had flown in to catch a game and continue those discussions in person.

I had a chance to talk to Mike after the game, and I told him I thought he had an incredible story. To return to college and finish his long-delayed senior season of football after nearly four decades was amazing to me. Here was a grandfather who was eight years older than his head coach and had two children older than any of his teammates!

Reading Mike's story reminded me a lot of my own story. I had many obstacles to overcome in my youth, and like Mike, I always believed that one day my dreams would come true. Still, there are so many people across the country who need what Mike has to offer in this book to help them win their own personal battles. I am about the same age as many of Mike's most recent college teammates, so I can relate to the impact he had in their lives. I know that in my busy life, someone might tell me something valuable and it may go in one ear and out the other. But when you tell me a great story, you have my attention. That's what Mike does so well in his book. He's a great storyteller, and that's how he gets his point across and makes it stick.

The Senior is not a book written for any specific age group. This is a book for everyone, both young and old. This is not a book just about football either. Football is the game that makes the story possible, but Mike's inspirational story is about so much more than football. The challenges Mike addresses in his book are helpful not only for teams but for people from all walks of life. Mike's message hits home. It's about believing in yourself and understanding how that confidence impacts everyone around you . . . overcoming regret and turning a negative experience into a positive . . . understanding that fitness and mental preparation are important for all ages, so when opportunity knocks you can open that door.

Even as a professional athlete I know that to stay at the top of my game I can never forget the fundamentals I learned along the way. Almost everyone has some degree of influence in other people's lives. Mike tells you how to apply some basic fundamentals that allow you to maximize that influence so that you help not only others but yourself in the process.

This is not just a feel-good story. This is a story of redemption and giving back.

— LeBron James

ONE THE GREATEST REGRET

Have you ever done something you would give anything to be able to change, or at least forget? Something you rewind and replay a thousand times in your memory, and the awful ending is always the same?

It had been thirty-six years since I left Sul Ross University and my football team in Alpine, Texas. Actually, I didn't leave voluntarily; I was kicked out of school and off the team. The circumstances surrounding that August 1971 event were so personally painful that I had barely kept in touch with many of the teammates who had, up until that moment, been as close as family.

Life, as they say, goes on.

For the almost four decades since I was escorted out of Alpine, my life had been good. I was blessed with a wonderful family and had a beautiful home in Tennessee. I had discovered a faith in God that had helped me to manage, but not forget, my past. The part of my past I just couldn't shake was the loss of my senior year of college football and what might have been.

Sometimes the most amazing things happen when you least expect them.

In April 2007, three of my former teammates—Stan Williamson, Randy Wilson, and Bill Roberts—called to tell me about a class reunion being organized by the Sul Ross Alumni Association. Bill said I really needed to come to San Antonio for the final weekend in June and see some of my old buds.

"I just don't have time," I said, using the familiar excuse of being swamped with growing my exercise equipment company.

The truth of the matter was, I did have time. But I had worked a lot of years shoveling excuses on the memory of what had happened in an attempt to bury it, and I wasn't eager to voluntarily allow those memories to resurface.

1

I'm not sure how most people deal with emotional pain, but I just didn't share mine. My reasoning was, if I talked about it, that would only make it worse. Besides, there were no "feel good" answers that would make it go away.

But Bill, Stan, and Randy continued to pressure me to show. Then my wife, Eileen, presented the final objection I couldn't overcome. She said, "You need to do this. I know you want to see those guys, and there is no reason for you not to go."

Maybe it was time to deal with the past.

I coordinated my flight with Randy's so we arrived in San Antonio around the same time. These guys had been some of my closest friends, and it had been a long time since I had seen them. I was excited about the reunion.

As I walked into the hotel, I was immediately thankful I had come. One by one, old friends and teammates refused to shake hands; they just grabbed me with a hug—and the fun started immediately. Bill Roberts walked in the hotel lobby, looked around the room at everyone, and asked, "Do I look bad too?" We all shared in a hearty laugh, and I was thinking how much I was going to enjoy this weekend, no matter what.

By Saturday afternoon my former teammates and I had gathered around the pool at the Holiday Inn on the famous River Walk. Cold beer was flowing in the hot Texas sun, and the old stories, like our memories, were larger than life.

Some of the stories were funny. Some—including those of rock climbing at Cathedral Mountain, chasing the Marfa ghost lights across the desert in Jeeps, ridiculous fourteen-hour road trips to Las Vegas, and great football moments—were hard for the wives and those near us to believe. But all of them ended in roars of laughter. Our bond was as strong as ever. I guess that is what makes reunions so special.

Then, it was bound to happen: the subject turned to my untimely exit. Everyone knew the president of Sul Ross had forced our head coach, Richard Harvey, to send me packing after getting in one too many fights. All my teammates knew that, back in the day, fighting was something I was good at and actually enjoyed. But they still wondered why that particular fight was the one that ended my college career.

Given my history and the couple of dozen other brawls I had been in, why was the fight with a teammate such a big deal?

I explained to them that the fight with the freshman player wasn't the problem. It was simply the straw that broke the camel's back. It had been the other altercations over the previous two years that had put me on the administration's radar. The fight with my freshman teammate was just one too many.

I took my turn and shared details of my life after Sul Ross. I had gone home to Odessa for a couple of weeks and then moved to Austin for a new start. I had gotten married, earned my degree, and had three wonderful children and one very special grandson. Most of my teammates were involved in coaching, and so they were aware I had been a strength and conditioning coach at Nebraska, Oregon, and Texas A&M.

Then, out of nowhere, it surfaced. I blurted out words I hadn't been prepared to say, but they were words that needed to be spoken.

"I've never told any of you guys how badly it hurt me to lose my senior year," I said as everyone turned quiet. "You have no idea how long I grieved and actually cried about the loss of that year. I have always felt as your captain and team leader that I let you guys down, and I'm sorry for that. And I wanted you to know it's been the greatest regret of my life."

There was a pause. It was as if everyone was caught off guard by my comments. I continued and shared more personal feelings.

"You know, what really gets me more than anything about all of it is that I still feel like I can play."

A lot of baby boomers might make a statement like that after a few beers and not really mean it. But I was dead serious. My comment was answered by laughter from everyone except Stan Williamson.

Stan stared at me and said, "Why don't you?"

I sat there and looked at Stan as that question buzzed in my head.

"*Why don't you?*"

It was like someone had told me I'd just won the lottery, but it really didn't register. After a few seconds I asked Stan, "Man, do you think I can do that?"

"Well, you didn't play anywhere else after you left, and I don't know, but I think you might have that senior year of eligibility remaining. You're in great shape. If you feel like you can run and take the hitting, and if that's your biggest regret, go back and do something about it."

My mind raced.

Could I be eligible? Could I go back to Sul Ross at fifty-nine years old and have another shot at my senior year?

Everyone around the pool talked, laughed, and enjoyed each other's company, but I was off in my own world.

Why don't you?

I couldn't get that question out of my head. Those words had challenged me. I had kept myself in good shape for years with my strength training and running. I knew I wasn't as fast as I used to be, but I wasn't slow either. I weighed two hundred pounds, about the same now as I did the last time I'd played thirty-six years ago, and I had never been hurt. I really believed I could play, and play well.

At dinner that night I grabbed one of my former teammates, Terry Stuebing, who had been an athletic director at several Texas high schools over the years. I couldn't quit thinking about going back to play, and I wanted to get as much information as possible before I called Eileen back at our home in Franklin, just outside of Nashville.

I leaned toward Terry and asked almost in a whisper, "Terry, is there any way I could still have eligibility left after all these years?"

Terry said he didn't know for sure, because when we played at Sul Ross, it was Division II, and now it was Division III. He told me he would do some checking when he got home, but what I really needed to do was contact the NCAA offices and have them give me that information.

I headed up to my room to call Eileen.

I thought about the timing of all of this. Our two oldest children were married and had started lives of their own. Our youngest daughter had just graduated from high school and was leaving in a few weeks for her freshman year in college. Since Eileen and I were "empty nesters," we had decided to downsize and put our house up for sale. Despite a slow market, we actually had already received a contract on it. I also had a young man, Jason Daniel, I could trust to run my business for me.

In my mind, I had all the answers—now if I could only convince my wife.

I telephoned Eileen. I told her I really didn't know anything for sure yet, but there was a chance I might still have some eligibility left at Sul Ross; if that was the case, I might be able to go back and play my senior year.

Silence . . . then, "Really?"

"Yeah," I said.

"We can talk more about it when I get home," I added as I quickly changed the subject.

I knew Eileen thought it was just my ego talking. I wanted to wait until I got home and contacted the NCAA before I said anything else to her about it.

Randy and I talked more football the next day. Randy said he had discussed it with Stan, and they both agreed that if there was anyone who could play college football at age fifty-nine, it was me.

Randy, ever the realist, offered his encouragement. "Hey bud, what's the worst that could happen? If you go out there and get your butt kicked and go home, no one will know. If that's the worst-case scenario, why not try?"

It had been a wonderful two days.

As Randy and I said our good-byes to everyone and left the hotel for the airport, I thought about how most of my former teammates were headed back to their normal routines without a lot of surprises in store. I, however, had a dream and a plan.

I might fail. I might even be embarrassed. But nothing would be worse than the pain of regret that I had suffered for the past thirty-six years.

I had to try.

TWO "MIKE, ARE YOU
IN JAIL?"

It was settled, at least in my mind. It wasn't the beer or an exaggerated pride in masculinity. I wasn't off my fifty-nine-year-old rocker either.

I knew I wanted to return to Sul Ross to play football—if I was still eligible nearly forty years after the fact. When I arrived home in Franklin from my football reunion in San Antonio, I immediately telephoned Jerry Larned.

A lot of time had passed since I was escorted out of Alpine by the graduate assistant coaches. Over the years I had tried to keep tabs on Coach Larned. One of my high school coaches, Leldon Hensley, and I had spoken in recent years, and he had told me that Coach Larned was in Abilene, Texas. Coach was the athletic director at McMurry State University, a Division III school that was in the American Southwest Conference along with Sul Ross and seven other schools that had football programs.

I called directory assistance, got a home number for Coach Larned, and made the call. His wife answered.

I said, "Hello, Mrs. Larned, this is Mike Flynt. Is Coach there?"

"Yes, Mike, he's standing right here." I heard her say, "Jerry, Mike Flynt is on the phone."

Coach picked up the phone, and the first words out of his mouth were, "Mike, are you in jail?" I smiled and answered, "Yes, Coach, that's why I'm calling." He laughed, and I told him that wasn't the case this time. Coach Larned had been my go-to guy and one of the coaches I called when I'd been in a fight and was in a bind with the Alpine police when I first attended Sul Ross. The truth was, I again needed his help, but for an entirely different reason.

"Coach, I am dead serious about something, and I have to ask you about it." I took a quick breath and fired away. "I want to return to Sul Ross and play football."

There was a pause. I am sure Coach had to clear his head for a moment, because he asked, "How old are you, Mike?"

I said, "I am fifty-nine."

Coach answered, "Well, I think you're crazy, but if you tell me you can play, I believe you."

I said, "Coach, I can play."

We talked a few more minutes. Coach, of course, reminded me that I wasn't twenty years old and that my plan sounded, well, a tad idiotic. But Coach also knew from Coach Hensley that I kept myself in great physical shape and that I was serious when it came to football.

Coach added that he'd love to have me at McMurry State, but I told him it had to be Sul Ross. It was Sul Ross or nothing. Coach said, "All right, here's what you need to do." He gave me the name of the person who handled NCAA rules and conference eligibility requirements at the American Southwest Conference offices in Richardson, Texas. I thanked Coach Larned and told him I deeply appreciated his help, as always.

I hung up, and the next call I made was to Amy Carlton at the American Southwest Conference.

When I reached Ms. Carlton, I told her Coach Larned had referred me. At first I tried to third-party it as if I had called on behalf of another person who wanted to return to school and play football. But it became too confusing as we discussed rules and regulations for different NCAA classifications and different conferences. Sul Ross was in the Division II Lone Star Conference when I played for the Lobos, but it had since been changed to the Division III American Southwest Conference.

Finally I said, "Look, it's me I'm talking about. I played thirty-seven years ago in 1970, and I got kicked off the team during two-a-days thirty-six years ago in 1971 before classes started. I had one semester of eligibility left back then, and I am just trying to find out if I still have that senior year of eligibility left."

She asked, "Well, do you have your transcripts with you?"

"Yes, ma'am, I do."

"All right, let's go through it semester by semester." We stayed on the telephone for about thirty minutes doing exactly that.

We reviewed each class and each semester and reviewed the NCAA rules that would apply to my situation. Then she read me Bylaw 14.1.9, which stated I had ten semesters to play four semesters. There were no time requirements and no age limit. Even though I had already received my degree, I had done so in nine semesters. I would need to enroll for at least nine hours as a graduate student to be considered a full-time student.

We finished going over everything, and Ms. Carlton said, "Okay, Mr. Flynt. How many years did you say it has been since you last played?"

I told her thirty-seven.

She answered, "Not only are you eligible, but I *will* come watch you play!"

I could scarcely contain my excitement. *So far, so good,* I thought to myself.

My next step was to contact Steve Wright, the fifty-one-year-old head football coach at Sul Ross. I telephoned a few times and left messages, but the only person I talked to was Sherry Strickland, the secretary in the athletic department. Finally, it hit me. I thought, *Man, there is no way I can break this news over the telephone. If I was the head football coach at Sul Ross and a fifty-nine-year-old guy called me and said he wanted to try out for my football team, hey, the answer would be easy.* Click, *I'd hang up the phone.*

I stepped out in faith. I purchased a plane ticket and flew into the Midland-Odessa Airport on July 12, 2007, jumped into a rental car, and drove the 160 miles southwest to Alpine. It was a drive I had made many times during my youth, but it was the first time in thirty-six years I had found myself on

I-20 West, Texas-18 South, and US-67 South. I was behind the wheel, and, in a way, headed back in time.

I counted the miles and recounted the memories.

I drove into Alpine and turned right off of East Holland Avenue into the parking lot next to the Sul Ross State Athletic Department. I found Coach Wright's office. He was behind his desk when I knocked on the door.

Coach Wright looked up and said, "Come in."

I was polite and straight to the point. I introduced myself and told him who I was and when I had been at Sul Ross before. I explained my conversations with Amy Carlton at the American Southwest Conference offices and that I had one semester of eligibility left. I told him that I had been a team captain and the leading tackler on the team. I explained I had been kicked off the team and out of school for fighting at the beginning of my senior year and I wanted a chance to try out for his football team.

Coach Wright just sat there and looked at me and finally said, "When did you play at Permian High School?" I said, "Well, it was forty-two years ago, 1965." And he said, "And how old are you?" I said, "I'm fifty-nine."

He said, "Gosh, man, I don't know."

Just about that time, assistant head coach Drew Bridges stepped inside Coach Wright's office and said, "Coach, we have a bunch of freshmen waiting on us down at the practice field."

Coach Wright looked at me and said, "Yeah, I've got a bunch of kids here for orientation. We're going to go down and see if they can run, see what kind of athleticism they have. So I've got to get down there and meet them."

I said, "Well, can I go down there with you?"

"Yeah," he replied. "Come on, you can ride with us."

So we started out of the offices, and Coach Bridges asked me, "Do you know a guy named Rich Barnes?"

I said, "Yeah, Rich played here when I played here. He was a defensive back when I was playing at linebacker."

Coach Bridges said, "He's my father-in-law."

Whoa! By this time I was really starting to feel dated.

South Texas weather in mid-July can be brutally hot, so I had worn nylon baggy pants and a T-shirt on the trip. When we reached the practice area adjacent to Jackson Field, the team's football stadium, Coach Wright instructed the seventeen freshmen players to stretch and get loose. I asked if I could join them. Coach Wright looked at me as if I was nuts but said, "Yeah, if you want to."

I jumped in and stretched out, and we selected teams for a flag football game. One team was shirts, and the other team was skins. I was on the skins team, so I peeled off my T-shirt. We played for about an hour. We ran mostly long, deep pass patterns. It was fast and it was hot. When our feet hit the ground, we could see the dust rise from the grass. Our only break was an easy jog back to the huddle between plays.

Finally, Coach Wright blew the whistle and told the freshmen, "You guys have got to get to orientation in about fifteen minutes; don't be late. Mike, come with me and I will take you back to your car."

When we got into his van, Coach Wright said, "Mike, this is a really good thing that you did, coming down here in person and doing this. This is a good thing, but I've got a million things going through my mind, and I need to sleep on this. I need you to meet me in the morning at nine thirty in my office, and I'll give you an answer."

I stayed at the Ramada Inn that night, and I was in Coach Wright's office at nine thirty sharp the next morning. I was more apprehensive than nervous. Assistant coaches Drew Bridges, Scott Howard, and Brandon Allen were in his office too.

Coach Wright, an average-sized man with blond hair and wire-rimmed glasses, looked at me and said, "All right, Mike, I'm going to give you a chance to make this team. I thought when I put you out there yesterday with those freshmen that it was going to cause complete chaos. A fifty-nine-year-old man out there with those eighteen-, nineteen-year-old kids. But man, you ran with them. You can run with them, and you just blended with them. I was up late last night thinking about this and got up early this morning weighing this in my mind.

"In my thought process there were really three questions that had to be answered before I could make this decision. Number one was, physically, could you do this at fifty-nine years old? There's no doubt in my mind that physically you're capable of doing this. And don't you ever take your shirt off around me again." We all laughed when he said that. Then he continued.

"Number two is a reason. There had to be a good reason for a fifty-nine-year-old guy to come back and do this. To be honest with you, I can't think of a better reason than what you've given me.

"And the third thing is a passion. Do you have the desire it will take to do this? I think you've probably got more desire than any player on this team. I hear it in your voice; I see it in your eyes. So you be here for two-a-days on August 12 and be ready to go."

Coach Wright then added his first stipulation, one that I really didn't think anything of when he initially mentioned it: "I don't want anyone to know you are coming down here to try out." I told him I had contacted some of my former teammates from Permian and Sul Ross and told them about this trip, but that was it.

He said, "That's okay; I'm talking about the press. If the press gets hold of this, we will have a media circus on our hands."

I assured him I wouldn't talk to the press about coming back to play. I really didn't think there would be that much interest in me playing football anyway. But I quickly realized that the interest was already starting to build.

I shook hands with Coach Wright and the assistant coaches and thanked each one of them. Coach Bridges gave me a workout manual—I had less than a month before I had to return for the start of workouts. I was ecstatic. I telephoned Eileen and told her Coach Wright was going to give me an opportunity, and I was headed back to the Midland-Odessa Airport to fly home.

Eileen said, "All right, we'll talk about it when you get home."

I also telephoned Stan Williamson—my former Sul Ross teammate and good friend who had challenged me at our reunion to return to Sul Ross—and told him the news. Stan was excited too. He told me he had thought about going back himself for years. He told me again, "If anyone can do it, you can." I wanted to believe that. I was going to give it my best shot.

I don't remember a lot about the return flight home. My mind was on football, the past—and redemption.

_____

The timing seemed so perfect. Our two oldest children were married and our youngest daughter, Lily, was headed to the University of Tennessee in Knoxville for her freshman year. We had decided to sell our home and downsize. We had a house and five acres in the woods outside of Franklin. It was gorgeous, but the upkeep took too much time and work. We figured a smaller home would better fit our empty-nest lifestyle. We listed the house on the market, and within ten days we had a contract.

I also didn't have any upcoming business obligations with our company, Powerbase Fitness. We had switched our manufacturing plant from Taiwan to China, and the transition had delayed our distribution schedule until late fall or early next year.

Had the opportunity to return to Sul Ross happened a year earlier, I could not have chased this dream. Sure, I could have said all the same things—"I need to go do this because . . ."—but I would not have had the time and flexibility. We had this big house and yard to take care of. Lily was a senior in high school, and I had business obligations with Powerbase scheduled at high schools in different areas of the country.

I would have thought, *Man, I would love to try and do this, but I just can't. I can't do this to Lily; I can't do this to Eileen; and I can't do this to my business.* But the way everything was happening now, it couldn't have been more perfect. I was thinking there is nothing, no reason, to keep me from making this happen.

I had one last major hurdle to overcome before I could head to Alpine.

For the past two months Eileen had been totally wrapped up in getting the house prepared to sell and keeping it show-ready. Now we had a contract and she was packing and thinking about where we were going to move, and also getting Lily all set to take off for her freshman year in college. She already had hotel reservations for Parents' Weekend at UT and plans for us to attend their first home football game in Knoxville. She wasn't thinking a lot about me playing football. In fact, she hadn't seriously considered it at all.

Eileen had a list of available homes that she wanted us to go see. She wanted to move into a home as quickly as possible after we closed on the house. I began to explain to her that Coach Wright had given me a chance to try out for the team at Sul Ross and I had to take advantage of that opportunity. That's when the frustration surfaced and Eileen said, "I cannot believe that at fifty-nine years old you are thinking about going back to play college football! I feel like I'm married to Peter Pan!"

Then it hit me. *Eileen doesn't understand how important this is to me.* I told her, "If I go back and try to make the team and can't make it, I can live with that. I will give it my best shot, and that will be the end of it. But to have a chance to go back and make the team and not even try would be worse for me than it was the first time when I was kicked out."

I had never told Eileen how badly it hurt me to lose that senior year and how much I regretted letting my teammates down. I had shared with each of our children, at different times in their lives, about the regret I had over the loss of that senior year. For each of them it had been used as a teaching tool regarding consequences for our actions. I wanted them to know there are always consequences for our actions, good or bad.

I told Eileen, "I know I can't do anything about what happened thirty-six years ago. The past is the past and I can't change that. But if I can make this team and make any contribution at all to a bunch of young guys I don't even know, then, for me, it makes up for those guys I let down so long ago."

For the first time in our thirty-five-year marriage, Eileen realized how much losing that senior year meant to me and how important it was for me to take this chance. She finally gave in and said, "Well, okay, let's go play football. Maybe it will be a great adventure; you've been talking about taking me back to Alpine for years. Also, it will definitely help me deal with the empty-nest syndrome!" Eileen had talked recently about how we had been raising our children for thirty-three years now, and she needed to have a plan when our last "baby" left home.

Now we had plenty to do in a short period of time.

I felt awesome physically, but I knew my body needed additional strength to absorb the pounding and punishment that comes from playing football. Each morning for about thirty minutes I incorporated more heavy strength training that complemented my Powerbase workouts.

I also increased the intensity of my sprint workouts to maximize my speed and better condition my leg muscles for football. My body weight had not fluctuated more than ten pounds over the years. I still weighed two hundred pounds, even though I had actually lost an inch from my five-foot-eleven frame over time due to the normal aging process and my many years of heavy weight training.

I had been blessed to have never suffered a serious joint injury on or off the football field, and the last time I was sick was when I had bronchitis as a twelve-year-old. I was young at heart and lived by the adage, "How old would you be if you didn't know how old you were?" Honestly, I would've been thirty-two because that's how I felt.

More importantly, I had my family and my faith.

Eileen and I tied up loose ends concerning the house. We signed the paperwork and closed on the house on August 6. We put almost everything we owned into storage. I started the twelve-hundred-mile drive to Alpine the following day. Everything I needed was in the U-Haul I pulled behind my truck.

I was headed back to college.

Eileen was scheduled to arrive in Texas a couple of weeks later. She was going to stay behind in a hotel and move Lily into school for her freshman year, then fly out. We had decided we could share my truck during the five-month quest.

The first challenge I knew I had to overcome when I arrived at Sul Ross was being accepted by my much younger teammates. I knew this would be strange for them, seeing a fifty-nine-year-old man trying out for their team. I really didn't know how I would accomplish this, or even if it could be accomplished.

The start of practice was August 12, but I had to report early for my physical. I arrived in Alpine around two in the afternoon on August 8, and I headed to the football offices to check in and pick up my paperwork.

I knocked on Coach Wright's door. He looked up and said, "Come in. How was your trip?" Then he leaned over and yelled to Coach Bridges in his office across the hall, "I need to take that NCAA test. How do I get online to do that?" The pair hollered back and forth as I sat on a sofa in Coach Wright's office.

Coach Wright started his test that reviewed NCAA rules and didn't say a word to me for the next fifteen minutes or so. I sat there and thought, *I have a lot of things I need to do. I have to find a place to live.* I got up and told Coach Wright that I needed to leave, and he said, "Okay, we'll get a schedule for you." I asked about my physical form, and he told me where to go and who to call.

I walked out and thought, *Man, Coach Wright isn't too talkative.*

Then, as I thought about it, I remembered when I was at Sul Ross nearly forty years ago, the last thing I wanted to do was hang out with the coaches. If I walked into a restaurant in Alpine and saw some of the coaches in there, I turned around and walked out. I didn't want to be around them. I thought this time shouldn't be any different. I didn't want to be friends with Coach Wright and his assistants; they were the coaches and I was a player.

I also thought about the conversation Coach Wright and I had when we'd met in his office a month earlier. Even then he was concerned that any media attention generated by my return to Sul Ross might disrupt his practices. In fact, it was only a few days after our first visit, when I returned to Franklin, that Coach Wright telephoned and wanted to know if I had talked to or alerted the media. Word had started to spread about my story and return to Sul Ross. I guess one of my former teammates had mentioned it to someone, and things have a way of getting around. I said, "No, I certainly have not."

Coach Wright said he had been contacted by a writer from the *Houston Chronicle,* and he told the writer, "There will be no cameras on the practice field, and you cannot come down here and interview Mike." The reporter said he intended to fly to Nashville to meet with me. "If that's where Mike Flynt is, I am going up there. I am going to cover this story whether you like it or not."

That didn't go over well with Coach Wright, and he was extremely upset. He said, "I told my staff that if I found out any of them had been leaking information, they'd be fired. I will fire them." I sat there and thought, *You are going to fire one of your assistant coaches over something getting out about me coming back and playing football?* I could not believe it. I honestly thought he might withdraw his offer to let me try out before I left Franklin for Alpine.

"I am not going to go back on my word," Coach Wright continued, "but this media thing is already getting out of hand."

When he made that statement, it was almost like our relationship had changed 180 degrees from the first time we met and he'd said, "Mike, this is a really good thing that you did, coming down here in person and doing this."

I was beginning to wonder how he felt about things now.

THREE I DIDN'T FALL FAR
FROM THE TREE

In order to really understand who I am, one has to understand who I came from and how their experiences, philosophies, and lives shaped my own.

My story started on both sides of the Atlantic. My father was a farm boy from Mississippi and my mother was his "English Rose," the bride he brought home after World War II. Their story is romantic, tragic, and inspiring.

James Vardeman—everyone called him J. V.—grew up outside of Hattiesburg, Mississippi, in a small community called Mount Olive. There were four boys and four girls in his family (he was the third son), and everyone had a role to play on the farm. Besides working the fields, Dad learned as much as he could about woodworking and cabinet crafting in hopes he could leave the farm one day.

Dad's family had little use for schooling; he dropped out after the third grade. The extra pair of hands on the farm was more important to his parents than the education, so he stayed home and worked. He learned the land and dealt with the elements at an early age. These were skills that served him well on the battlefields of Europe and in the West Texas desert years later.

When World War II broke out, Dad was only nineteen years old. But like so many young men of that generation, he enlisted in the army and headed to Europe. It might have been a lonely time—to go from being surrounded by a big family to suddenly being alone—but his best friend, Hayes Lee, enlisted with him. The two left for basic training together before being shipped to different places in England.

Mother, Pat (Lillian Patricia), grew up in northern England in Nottingham, the town famous for its beloved outlaw son Robin Hood. Her father was a post-man and her mother was a homemaker who died while giving birth to my mother's youngest brother, Bill. Mom was still very young but had to assume most of the responsibilities for taking care of her brothers and sister. She had a very close friend, also named Patricia, with whom she spent most of her spare time when she wasn't involved in daily chores. Life was hard, but nothing like it was going to be once Hitler started bombing England.

With the onset of the war, Mom joined the Women's Land Army and was part of a brigade that cut down trees to clear land for the airports and landing strips that were becoming necessary in their part of the country. Felling trees and then chopping the limbs off the trunk with a hand ax was very hard work. It's no wonder Mom worked as hard as she did all the years I was growing up. Some things just don't change—she is still working hard today at eighty-two years old, up to forty hours a week at her job.

When the American GIs rolled into England in the early spring of 1944, they camped just outside of Nottingham. One night, at a dance hosted for the WLA members and United States servicemen, my dad spotted my mother. Dad later told me, "She looked like a beautiful porcelain doll." Dad always said he knew right then and there that he would marry that girl. Mom always laughed about Dad's remarks that night and said, "Once I met him, I couldn't get rid of him!"

In fact, Dad managed to get in a fight that first night they met when a certain sailor kept trying to get my mother's attention. Dad finally got sick of it and called him out.

The fact that I exist can tell you who won that scuffle!

Dad was part of the 28th Infantry that left Nottingham for Normandy just after the first wave of the D-Day invasion and later pressed into Germany in the Battle of the Bulge. But he didn't know any of that was on the horizon at the time. He just saw a beautiful, energetic young woman whom he couldn't get out of his mind. Mom often said she thought Dad was the most handsome guy she'd ever seen. They started seeing each other regularly, and in May 1944, after only a few months of courtship, they were married. They had only a few brief weeks together before he was shipped out to Southampton, England, and then to France in June.

Things obviously weren't as pleasant for my dad on the other side of the channel. The 28th fought in the infamous hedgerows for the region, pushing on into German territory deeper in France and along the Luxembourg border as autumn set in. The American and British troops were able to move forward much more quickly than anyone had anticipated. While this was, of course, a good thing, it also presented a number of problems that no one had anticipated. The primary one was a lack of supplies.

By October the situation was dire and the Allied armies halted their advance in order to regroup and try to make adjustments. Unfortunately, this gave the Germans a chance to regroup as well. Hitler was especially interested in stopping the progress on the western front because he hoped to cause the British and American forces to seek a treaty with him, which would allow him to concentrate his efforts and resources in the east by taking down the Soviets. He underestimated the Allied fighting force, however, and the dream team of their commanding generals: the British had General Montgomery; the Americans had Generals Eisenhower, Bradley, and Patton; and the assembled troops outnumbered the Germans by more than three hundred thousand.

The one element the Allies didn't have on their side was the weather. The snow fell heavy and fast, and the temperatures dropped as winter arrived. By the time the showdown started, it was already mid-December. The fighting rolled into late January. The troops were scattered throughout the hilly forests of Germany, Belgium, and Luxembourg. Soldiers suffered from the fierce elements as much as from the fierce German resistance and heavy firepower.

Some of the worst fighting was in the center of the region, where the 106th and my dad's 28th Infantry Battalion were stationed. The Germans made some headway there, and estimates of Allied casualties ranged from seven thousand to nine thousand. It was one of the most devastating fronts in the European theater toward the end of the war.

My father was among the many who were wounded. Forced to withdraw under cover of darkness, Dad and some of his buddies had to wade across a shallow creek that was nearly waist deep. Once across, however, they couldn't build a fire out in the open for fear that it would alert German artillery. He and his fellow soldiers dug trenches into the snow and lit fir tree branches in an attempt to keep warm and safe, but it did little to help.

Dad's legs froze.

He was able to keep moving the next day, but the damage had been done. After several more days of fighting, his legs bothered him so much that he was unable to maneuver effectively and was sent to the rear for his own safety. While he did regain use of his legs through physical therapy after the war, he would always complain of pain in his legs and would eventually lose one of his legs toward the end of his life.

Even so, Dad was one of the lucky ones. He was alive.

Dad was shipped back to England, where he was eagerly met by my mother and his new baby daughter, Patricia Ann, who'd been born only weeks earlier.

Dad, Mom, and Ann rode out the rest of the war in England until Dad was shipped back to the States with the army. It was a sad and tearful departure. Mom and Ann were unable to accompany him on his trip back because of the amount of paperwork involved for their clearance. It was more than a year before Mom left England to be with him.

Back in America, Dad worked to repair his body so he would be able to provide a life for his young family as soon as they could join him. He was lonely for his wife and daughter, but he was also looking forward to the day when they were cleared to emigrate across the Atlantic Ocean.

It wasn't until June 1946 that Mom's paperwork finally cleared. Mom left baby Ann at home with a babysitter and went into town to send Dad that much-anticipated cable—she and Ann were ready to set sail. While Mother was in town to wire the great news, however, the unthinkable happened. Ann, who was eighteen months old, wandered out of the house and into the street. She was hit by a dump truck and killed instantly.

Dad later told me that he received two cables that same day. The first one said Mom and Ann would be leaving the next day for America. The second informed him that his precious baby girl had been killed. Mom stayed in England long enough to bury Patricia Ann and then set out alone, with empty arms and a broken heart, to start a new life in America.

I was about eight years old when I finally got up enough courage to ask Mom about the picture of the pretty little blonde-haired, blue-eyed girl that sat on her dresser. I had noticed the picture for years but just never really thought much about it until one day it dawned on me that I had no idea who that little girl was or why her picture was sitting on my mom's dresser.

Mom told me the story, and I was heartbroken for her and Dad. I think it was that day I began to look at my mom differently. I began to realize how special she was to have endured what she did and to have made the sacrifice to move to a foreign country and leave everything and everyone she knew behind.

———————

Mom was a resilient woman, and she soon found that America was a fascinating place to be and a good place to start over. She joined Dad in Mississippi and marveled at how readily available everything was. In England, people had lived under rationing for much longer than they had in America, and many items hadn't returned to their prewar availability nearly as quickly as they had on this side of the Atlantic. There were a number of times while I was growing up when Mom said she felt a bit guilty at how easily she was able to attain everything from staple items such as meat and butter to "luxury" items such as stockings.

Mom enjoyed her new life in America, but she still grieved for Ann and missed her family back in England. In an effort to ease some of her loneliness, she sent a letter to her childhood friend, Patricia, with whom she had fallen out of touch. Mom had hoped to hear where Patricia's life had led her. Well, it turned out that it hadn't led her very far from Mom at all.

In fact, in one of those amazing things that can only be explained as one of God's mysteries, Mom's best friend, Patricia, was also a war bride. She had met and married Hayes Lee, Dad's best friend who had enlisted in the army with him, and the two planned to return to Mississippi.

But it doesn't end there.

Several years later, Patricia's younger sister, Enid, arrived from England for a quick visit. Enid met Dad's younger brother, Terrell, and he and Enid fell in love and were married. Mom desperately needed a friend and a familiar face; she got more than she ever could have dared to hope. I know Mom was grateful for Patricia's presence in her life.

Mom and Dad decided to make a life for themselves in Mississippi, and soon started a family.

First there was my older sister, Gwendolyn, in 1947, and then I came along one year later. Our younger sister, Pamela, was born five years later in 1953. We stayed close to Pearl, Mississippi, and were surrounded by many of my father's lifelong friends and our family. Dad worked at Easley & Easley making cabinets, while Mom worked as a waitress at a local diner.

Nearly all my memories from that period involve my grandparents on my dad's side. Mother told me that I even learned to walk in the hallway of their home. Many years later I took Eileen back to Mississippi to the very house that my grandparents lived in when I was a child. The house was vacant, but we still got inside. The hallway where I learned to walk, that I remembered as being like a highway in size, seemed so small and narrow. I guess that just happens when you go back to someplace where you haven't been since you were a kid.

I was very close to Grandpa Flynt, who loved to play outdoors with me and let me run wild on the farm whenever I stayed with them. I was pretty sure my mother was grateful, since I always returned home tired and ready for a nap. That wonderful farm was every little boy's dream come true. There were woods and trails and all kinds of farm animals. There was a big barn with a loft. Grandpa Flynt was in total control and knew everything about everything.

A perfect example of this happened one day that I remember so vividly. Grandpa Flynt warned me not to go down by the creek near the blacktop road that ran in front of their home. He had spotted some snakes down there and told me that I needed to steer clear of that area so I wouldn't get bitten.

Of course, the first thing I had to do was go down to the creek myself to see if what he said was true. It was.

Even as I stood at what I thought was a safe distance away from the water, a huge water moccasin started up the side of the bank and came slithering toward me. I froze from fear and just started screaming as loudly as I could. Almost as soon as I opened my mouth, there was a shotgun blast from behind me as Grandpa shot that snake in about four pieces. Knowing me as he did, he had followed me right out of the house and down to the creek, carrying his shotgun with him. From that day forward there was never anything else that he warned me not to do that I didn't mind to the letter.

The early 1950s was a boom time for West Texas and its newly discovered oil fields, so the Flynts and the Lees decided to head out West. I guess Dad figured that where the economy was booming there would be jobs, and where there were jobs there would be families needing homes, and those homes would need cabinets. Our family packed and left the rich farmland of Mississippi and headed for the mesquite-covered desert of Odessa.

I think my mother always preferred Mississippi to West Texas. Maybe the Southern charm reminded her of how things were in England, or maybe it just wasn't so dusty with the wind blowing all the time. But whatever the case, she always trusted my dad unwaveringly and never complained—that was just who she was. She'd followed him to America, so following him out to Texas was a small obstacle compared to that. The Lees were coming too, so Mom wouldn't be nearly so lonely with this move. Plus, Mom always threw herself completely into her work and managed to work her way to the top wherever she happened to be.

Mom is, without a doubt, the hardest worker I have ever known.

Never one to shirk responsibility, complain, or pass the buck, Mom attacked every challenge that came her way with confidence and a naturally pleasant disposition. Mom never forgot the hard times she suffered through when she was young. She looked at each day as a gift filled with hope and possibilities. If attitude is everything, then Mom had it all. Positive, aggressive energy tempered by kindness will get you a long way, and Mom combined those traits like no one I have ever known. Any leadership qualities that I may have, I learned from watching her.

Dad was a lot like Mom in many ways, but I was told that the war had changed him as it had so many young men in that day and time. He was tough and determined, and he and Mom made a great team.

My parents lived humble lives. But they did so with real pride in what they accomplished through hard work and a commitment to excellence that always impressed my sisters and me. These were the lessons that would stay in my mind and shape so much of my life as a husband, father, and athlete.

There was something else about Odessa that seemed to fit right into Dad's way of thinking. It was a passion that was shared by many throughout the state of Texas, but nowhere more than it was in Odessa.

That was the love of football.

FOUR BACK IN THE DAY

Knowing how my dad was raised and what he experienced in World War II, I understand much of his reasoning for training me like he did. And Dad was right about what I faced as I grew up in West Texas. It was tough, and so were the people. Dad included.

I was around twelve years old when Mom and Dad argued one night. Dad had been drinking at the American Legion, and Mom was upset with him. I was in the kitchen, right in the middle of the war of words. Dad was angry with Mom, but he took his frustrations out on me. He said something I never forgot.

"And you," he said, looking square at me, "you are a runt, and that's all you're ever gonna be is a runt."

Mom and I stared at Dad, who just stood there expressionless. It was like he was ashamed of what he had just said, so he simply turned and walked outside. In bed that night I made up my mind I would do everything I could to be bigger and stronger. I was not going to be a "runt."

The next day I clipped an advertisement by Charles Atlas from one of my comic books. Charles Atlas marketed a fitness program that he said developed his body from that of an "89-pound scrawny weakling" into a huge muscleman.

I was sold.

I took five dollars out of my mother's purse, rode my bike down to the mailbox, and sent for a workout program. That was the beginning of what would become a lifelong quest to be bigger and stronger and to stay in shape. Yes, I was small for my age. In fact, when I received my first Texas driver's license at age fifteen, I was all of five foot three and weighed 104 pounds.

But no way was I going to be a runt like Dad had said.

I wasn't going to let it happen.

In 1963, the summer before my sophomore year at Permian High School, Dad purchased fifteen acres outside of Odessa. Fifteen acres is not a lot of land unless you have to clear those fifteen acres of mesquite trees by hand.

A mesquite tree is actually not a tree but more like a bush. It's a native plant of the dry climate in West Texas. Like most of the native plants and shrubs in West Texas, the mesquite is covered with thorns. These aren't ordinary thorns, though; these are long enough and tough enough to pierce a brand-new tire just like a nail.

Dad paid a guy seventy-five dollars to go over the acreage with a special machine and cut the taproots on each of the mesquites. Those taproots could tunnel down twenty feet or more looking for water. It was essential to cut that root to kill the bush or it would just grow back. Having cut the taproots, this guy wanted another seventy-five bucks to use his equipment to pull, pile, and burn the mesquites.

Dad looked at me and said, "We can save that seventy-five dollars, and you and me will pull these mesquites ourselves."

Dad's fifteen acres were totally covered with mesquite. Some of the bushes were six and seven feet high. Cutting the taproot made it possible to pull the mesquite by hand, but because of all the feeder roots, it was anything but easy.

Wearing jeans, boots, and long-sleeve shirts in 100-degree temperatures, Dad and I tackled the mesquites. Working by myself during the week and with Dad's help on weekends, it took the entire summer to clear the land.

First, we waded very carefully into the mesquite. We separated the limbs, pushed back the thorns, and grabbed the biggest part of the trunk we could—as close to the ground as possible—and we pulled. The mesquite started to come out of the ground, but the feeder roots would sometimes be ten, fifteen, and twenty feet long. We pulled and pulled until all the roots came out of the ground. We piled and burned the brush, and man, was it oven-hot work! I later learned that when you put mesquite wood in a fireplace with a conventional iron grate, the heat from the burning mesquite will melt the grate.

It was some of the hardest work I had ever done, but it was great exercise. I mean, it worked my back, legs, hips, shoulders, and arms better than a gym could have. It also worked my attitude. I had to prepare mentally every day to take on that job. I pulled, piled, and burned mesquite the whole summer. I grew an inch or two taller, but more important, I gained more muscle in less time than I ever had before, or have since. By the end of the summer, as I stood with my shirt off in front of the mirror, I was so glad that Dad had decided to save that seventy-five dollars.

Dad's plan once we had the land totally cleared was to sow alfalfa and hope that we could grow enough to feed the horse he had bought and maybe have a little left over to sell. We soon learned that Odessa wasn't the garden spot of the West.

Odessa is located halfway between Dallas–Fort Worth and El Paso on Interstate 20 in the heart of West Texas. The city was born in 1871 when the Texas & Pacific Railroad Company, which had been chartered by Congress to build a railroad line from Marshall, Texas, to El Paso, pitched a camp at milepost 296.

History has it that the name Odessa was selected for the "future great city" after Odessa, Russia, then a prosperous and widely known wheat and wheat-seed center and seaport. This name would by synonymous to "wheat country" in the sales pitch made to farmers in the North and Midwest.

"The future city" was described as being on "the Staked Plains of West Texas," with sunshine, pure water, and "no mosquitoes or dengue fever." To overcome the fear of the West, prospective investors were assured there were "no Indians nearer than three hundred miles, there has never been a Mexican raid," and the "cowboys (are) as peaceful as gentlemen." I haven't met that particular "cowboy" as of yet.

Odessa was actually a small ranch town until the oil boom, and that quickly changed everything. When huge oil reserves were discovered just to the south of Odessa, the area was quickly transformed into a large and growing oil center with refineries and plants that produced fuels, chemicals, plastics, industrial gas, and machinery.

When we moved to Odessa in the early 1950s, I was still very young. But it was easy to tell things were a lot different than they had been in Mississippi. There were cowboys everywhere, and lots of men who looked like they had been cleaning greasy driveways with their clothes. Dad told me those guys were oil-field hands and were known as "roughnecks."

The house we first lived in when we moved to Odessa was in a lower income area, and a lot of our neighbors were roughnecks. Roughnecking in those days was really dangerous work. It was a tough group to have your family around, so Dad decided to buy us a new home. And he did, right in the middle of a new area in north Odessa that was zoned for a new high school in the next few years. That school was Permian High.

Dad never played sports, but he told me that he thought he might have been a really good football player. Dropping out of school so early to work on the family farm eliminated any chances he had of being involved in organized sports. But he spent hours with me in our yard on East 35th Street throwing the baseball or football.

I picked up on Dad's love of football, and it quickly became my favorite sport. Children played organized football early in West Texas, and I was in full pads by the time I reached the third grade at Burnet Elementary.

Coach Keith, our football coach at Burnet, had just received three brand-new helmets. He called our team together before practice started one day, showed us the helmets, and told us they would be given to the three guys on our team who distinguished themselves as "headhunters." I immediately knew I had to win one of those helmets, and I did.

Glen Halsell and Tony Conley won the other two helmets. Glen was one of the football captains on our state championship team at Permian and was named All-American at linebacker. He played linebacker for the University of Texas and was an All-American for the Longhorns too. Tony also was on our state championship team at Permian and played his college football at Rice University in Houston.

Many of the players from our elementary team stayed in football, and we practiced and played together for years. Permian High School opened in 1959. I was in the sixth grade at the time, but I knew exactly where I would play high school football.

Odessa High School was the city's main high school prior to Permian's opening. Odessa High was established in 1908 and won Texas state football championships in 1944, 1945, and 1946. The school later had to forfeit the 1944 and 1945 titles because several of the players were ruled ineligible due to their World War II service.

Odessa's star player during that time was Hayden Fry. He played safety and quarterback, and everyone in town knew his name. In Hayden's senior season in 1946, Odessa won fourteen consecutive games, scored nearly four hundred points, and allowed around fifty points. One of the most amazing statistics from that season was that Odessa did not commit a single turnover the entire season.

Hayden Fry was the speaker at our high school football banquet in the spring of 1966. At that time he was the head football coach at Southern Methodist University in Dallas, and he and his teammates from the 1946 Odessa High championship team were our guests at the banquet. This was their twenty-year reunion, and I remember looking at those guys and thinking I didn't see how they ever could have played football; they sure looked old. It's funny how time has a way of changing the way you look at things.

It was in a hectic moment after our banquet that my dad and Coach Mayfield met briefly for the first time. Everyone was milling around; they shook hands, and Coach Mayfield asked my dad, "What did you ever do to make that kid so tough?" I heard the question, but I didn't hear how Dad answered in all the excitement.

I've always wondered how Dad answered that question.

———

When Permian opened for classes in 1959, 1,159 students from northern Odessa were enrolled. The school received its name from the Permian Basin, the geological formation on which Odessa is located. Permian's first football team that year was coached by Jim Dawson. The Panthers lost their first three games and finished the season at 4-6. Coach Dawson won twenty-one games in three seasons before Jim Cashion took over as head coach in 1962.

Permian had some truly great athletes in those early years, but the program was only average. In West Texas, where football is concerned, average is never going to cut it. Coach Cashion was fired after three seasons and a 15-15 record. Permian wanted a coach who could maximize, develop, and motivate the deep talent pool that was there at the school. The administration found their man in Coach Gene Mayfield.

The school hired Coach Mayfield prior to my senior year in 1965. Mayfield had played quarterback at West Texas State University and had begun his head-coaching career in Littlefield, Texas, before moving to Borger, Texas, in 1958. Coach Mayfield's 1962 Borger team made it to the Class 4A state championship game but lost 30-26 to San Antonio Brackenridge.

Coach Mayfield was a no-nonsense coach. I had no way of knowing it at the time, but from the first day I met him, I always measured every football coach I had against Gene Mayfield. And believe me, he set the bar pretty high.

Coach Mayfield walked into our very first meeting and said he had been told that the Permian players had the reputation as "the country club set." I had no clue what he was talking about, but when Coach explained himself I quickly understood. He said, "You guys sit out by the pool, drink beer, and talk about how good you are at football. From this day forward, there will be no more of that." Then he added, "We are going to be a defensive football team, because if they don't score, they can't beat us."

I was impressed with Coach Mayfield, but he really got my attention when he ended the meeting with this statement: "Everybody in this room is going to have a chance to be a starter on this team. I don't care who started in the past; everyone will have to earn a starting position."

That was music to my ears. Coach Cashion had always selected his top players even before practice started. I knew as a five-foot-eight, 132-pound junior, I was never going to measure up to his standards, literally. But now, with Coach Mayfield and the new assistants he brought with him, I had something to train toward. I was going to get a chance, and I made up my mind I would take advantage of it.

Training was always on my mind. I was constantly thinking of ways to get stronger and gain weight. I carried food everywhere with me, and I did something physical from the time I got up each morning until I went to bed each night. And like the summer before, I began to grow again.

I grew three inches and gained eighteen pounds of solid muscle in the spring and summer of 1965. I started two-a-days in the best shape of my life and was excited about the opportunity to finally contribute to our team.

Our team was thoroughly prepared for my senior season. Our confidence was in each other and our coaches. Coach Mayfield and his staff stressed discipline, on and off the field, and that was probably our secret weapon. No one gave us much of a chance at the beginning of that season. We were picked to finish somewhere in the middle of the District 2–Class 4A race, behind San Angelo and Big Spring, and I believe we were ranked sixty-fourth in the state.

As I had promised myself, I made the most of the chance Coach Mayfield gave me and earned a starting spot at defensive back and on special teams. And all of our hard work paid off in a big way: we won it all! Odessa Permian High School, 1965 Class 4A Football State Champions!

That first championship season was the beginning of a tremendous winning tradition at Permian High School that continues today and was the inspiration for the book, movie, and successful TV series, *Friday Night Lights*.

We had eighteen seniors on our championship team, and fourteen received college football scholarships. I had received offers from small colleges in New

Mexico and Oklahoma, but nothing that really interested me. I also received an offer from Sul Ross. I was excited about their offer but thought the school was too close to Odessa, and I really didn't want to go to college in a small town like Alpine. I wanted a big school and a big city. Most of my focus was on the Southwest Conference and other Division I programs.

I was fortunate enough to be one of five players from our team selected to the All-District team in District 2. At that time District 2, which was known as "The Little Southwest Conference," was the toughest in the state in Class 4A, which contained the largest schools in Texas. At 150 pounds, however, my lack of size concerned many Division I coaches. Coach Hayden Fry at SMU expressed interest in me, but he didn't offer me a scholarship. Honestly, I really wasn't worried about it. It would have been nice to receive a full ride at a Southwest Conference school, but I figured if I had to walk on to a team, that was okay because I had no doubt I could play at that level.

One day in February 1966, Coach Hensley, my defensive back coach at Permian, asked me to play in a half-line scrimmage later in the day. He told me they wanted to get a good look at returning players for next year. I was excited about the scrimmage because I loved everything about football, from practice to games.

One of our returning running backs was a junior named Billy Dale. We called him "Bulldog," and Billy was a great running back. With good speed at 190 pounds, Billy was an All-State selection the following year as a senior, and he played running back on the 1969 national championship team at the University of Texas.

As we started the drills, I noticed a former Permian coach, Melvin Robertson, had joined our coaches behind the offensive huddle. I had heard he was now the defensive coordinator at the University of Houston, but I had no idea why he was at this scrimmage. I thought he might have been in town on other business and decided to stop by and visit our coaches since they were friends.

The offense ran three plays, none of which was anything special.

Then it happened.

The quarterback dropped back into the pocket but then dipped down and handed the ball to Billy Dale on a draw play. I read it perfectly and had already started toward the line of scrimmage from my defensive back position. One of our defensive linemen broke through the line and hit Billy in the backfield, but Billy made one of his All-State running back moves and twisted out of the tackle.

As he did so, I timed it perfectly. I was at full speed when I unloaded everything I had into the middle of Billy's back. His head snapped back and the ball flew loose. We both went down in the backfield.

Coach Hensley blew the whistle, and I turned around and helped Billy up. As I walked back to the defensive side of the ball, I noticed Coach Robertson had started to walk away and was headed to the parking lot. I thought it was strange that he had visited with our coaches for only a few minutes.

The next morning I was in the cafeteria when Coach Hensley walked in and told me he had just received a phone call from Coach Melvin Robertson. Coach Robertson wanted to offer me a full scholarship to the University of Houston. I couldn't believe my ears. This was a dream come true! I had received the Division I scholarship that I needed for a chance to play at the next level.

It was twenty years later in 1985 at a Permian football reunion when Billy Dale mentioned that February 1966 scrimmage. He asked me if I remembered the tackle. I told him I did. He said, "I played my senior year at Permian and four years at the University of Texas, and I was never hit again as hard as you hit me that day." I smiled and told Billy that tackle earned me a full ride to the University of Houston.

After Coach Hensley gave me the great news about the University of Houston, I just knew my plans had finally come together. Or so I thought.

I dated a girl named Kay Mabry off and on in the last two years of high school. We had gotten pretty serious over the course of the football season and started to make plans for our future after graduation.

It was about the time I received the offer from Houston that Kay came up with a plan. We thought it was great, and it seemed to make more sense than me going off to Houston without her. Kay wanted to stay in Odessa and attend Odessa Junior College. My part was to attend a junior college close by and play football for two years, and then we could attend a college somewhere together.

Three of my good friends and Permian teammates—Danny Edwards, Phil Fouche, and Mike Conaway—had signed to play football on full scholarship at Ranger Junior College in Ranger, Texas. I talked with them briefly about the school and decided this would fit perfectly with Kay's and my plan.

I called Coach Jack Duvall at Ranger and heard the surprise in his voice when I told him I was interested in Ranger football. The program was only a few years old, but it was in the middle of a losing streak and eighty-five miles away from the nearest big city. He graciously told me that he had a full scholarship for me and he wanted me to join my teammates at Ranger.

That was it. Just like that, without ever visiting the school or talking with anyone else but Kay, I committed to Ranger Junior College. I am reminded of the saying, "Youth is wasted on the young."

This was the first, but certainly not the last, foolish decision I made over the next few years.

Between the distance from Odessa and the girls I started to meet at college, I quickly realized my relationship with Kay was over once I was away at school. There were so many other fish in the sea, but I was stuck at Ranger, and it had become a nightmare.

However, my teammates from Permian and a boyhood friend named Ronnie Ray, who also went to Ranger, made life bearable.

Off the field I spent a lot of time with one of our running backs from Harlem, New York, named Norman Smitherman. Nicknamed Smittie, he taught me to dance to the Motown sounds of Aretha Franklin, the Four Tops, Wilson Pickett, Stevie Wonder, and others. Mother taught me how to dance at an early age, and I had danced for years. I thought I was pretty good at it until I met Smittie. He was a great dancer. I watched and learned, and I still have fun dancing today.

On the field, I started at defensive back and on special teams. For me, Ranger was the means to an end. My plans in other areas had changed, but one thing hadn't changed: I was there to play football. But Permian High School it wasn't.

I couldn't believe I had come off a state championship football team to play for a team that wouldn't win a single game all year. Needless to say, the season was a disaster.

We had lost our nine previous games when we took on Henderson County Junior College. We were behind 45-0 when we looked to the sideline from our defensive huddle to get the signal for the next play. Coach Duvall looked at us with a stupid grin and just flipped us off. We were on our own.

Later in the game it looked like we were finally going to score. I was thankful we weren't going to be shut out. We were on the 2-yard line, and our quarterback threw a pass out in the flat to our wide receiver. But a defensive back for Henderson County stepped in front of our guy and intercepted the pass. He raced out of the end zone and sprinted down our sideline. He had nothing between him and the goal line but grass.

And me.

I stood on the sideline and watched him as he raced down the field on his way to an easy touchdown. I thought, *No way!*

I snapped my chin strap in place, came off the sideline, and nailed this guy with a picture-perfect tackle. The referee ran up, threw his flag, and hit me in the back as I walked back to the sideline. He said, "Number 25, you came off the bench!"

I thought that was the easiest call the ref had made all day. He picked up the ball, walked into the end zone, and awarded Henderson County a touchdown.

The newspaper headlines the next day read: "Ranger Junior College Uses 12 Men, Still Gets Beat 76-0."

I left Ranger at the end of that semester.

———————

During my time at Ranger I had stayed in close contact with Mike Campbell and Mike Paddock, two of my Permian teammates who were on football scholarships at the University of Arkansas. Our trainer at Permian, Jim Bone, had also taken a position as a trainer for the Razorbacks, and he was confident I had the ability to play for Arkansas. He had told me once at Permian that he thought Glen Halsell and I were the two toughest kids on that team. I was hopeful that he would share his opinion with the Arkansas coaches. I loaded up my car and headed for Fayetteville.

Football at Arkansas was not a problem for me; going to class was. I was told by Jim Bone that Martine Bercher, a former All-American defensive back for Arkansas, had watched me during spring drills and I was his favorite. I now weighed 172 pounds and loved being part of a big-time program in the Southwest Conference.

I met with Coach Broyles after spring practice, and he told me that he could give me a scholarship as soon as I was eligible after the transfer from Ranger. He also told me my grades needed to be a lot better. Coach Broyles's advice sounded good, but I was bound and determined to not let my education get in the way of my college experience.

Mom and Dad had borrowed money for me to go to Arkansas, and this was money that was not going to be repaid easily. I didn't want to ask them for more financial help, so I dropped out of school, and the coaches got me a job in Fort Smith, Arkansas. The money was great, and the plan was to save enough cash to pay for my next semester at Arkansas.

Once again, things did not go as planned.

Dad had broken his arm and was really having problems with work at his cabinet shop. He needed me to come home and help him, and so I did.

Things were different for me now in Odessa. I knew after only a few days that I did not want to stay; I needed to be playing football somewhere. I didn't know where—I just knew I needed to be ready.

The program at Arkansas had introduced me to some great training techniques for football, and I knew my part. I did what I had to do at my job, but my thoughts were always on training. There were many days and nights when I ran stadium steps and lifted weights in a local gym.

America was in the middle of the Vietnam War and the draft was in place in the mid-1960s. As long as you were a full-time college student, you were classified as 2-S, which was a college deferment from the draft. If you were eighteen years of age and not in college, you were classified as 1-A, which meant you were draft eligible.

When I dropped out of school at Arkansas in the spring of 1968 and moved back to Odessa, I was reclassified as 1-A. The U.S. Government wasted no time, and in the summer of 1968 they sent me a letter congratulating me that I had been "chosen" to serve in the United States Army. I had been drafted.

The Tet Offensive in Vietnam was one of the largest military operations ever organized; the plan was to put America in control of that war. To do that, they needed all the available men they could get, and I was being notified to report for my draft physical.

I was instructed to report to the bus station there in Odessa at 6:00 a.m. for a trip to Abilene for my physical. Much to my surprise, Mike Campbell was on that same bus. Mike was the quarterback and one of the captains from our state championship team at Permian, as well as one of my best friends. He attended the University of Arkansas on football scholarship but then decided he wanted to play baseball instead. He transferred from Arkansas to Pan American College in Edinburg, Texas. During the transfer he had also been reclassified as 1-A.

I knew this was going to be an interesting trip.

Mike hated the thought of anything and everything about the military. Don't get me wrong; he loved and supported our troops. He just didn't want to be one of them. I asked him what was in the large brown envelope he carried around. He showed me about a dozen X-rays of his back. I knew he had lower back problems, but I had no idea just how bad.

I laughed at Mike the entire trip. He was a nervous wreck. We had once gotten lost together for more than twelve hours in a cave in Arkansas before we finally found our way out, but I don't think he was as scared then as he was about this physical.

He worried for nothing, because the doctors in Abilene who handled the physicals were failing guys out on almost anything. One guy didn't pass because he had a rash on his back and doctors felt he probably couldn't carry a pack. Mike and his bad back were safe.

Of the fifty guys who made the bus trip that day, I think only seven of us passed our physicals. They took us into a small room, and we sat down at school desks. One of the officers walked to the front of the room and said, "Congratulations, you have each passed your physical and are qualified to serve in the U.S. Army."

He then asked our entire group, "Is there any reason why you shouldn't serve in this man's army?"

"Yes, sir," I said.

The other men turned and looked at me like I was crazy.

"I can't stand having someone telling me what to do all the time."

He laughed and said, "You'll make a good soldier."

As bad as I didn't want to admit it, I knew he was right.

We were told we would receive notice in the next two weeks to report for our induction physical, and then from there we would ship out to Fort Polk, Louisiana. Based on everything I had heard, we would depart from Fort Polk to Vietnam.

When I told Mom and Dad the news, their reaction was really predictable. Mom was worried about me, but like everything else in her life, she pretty much accepted it and took it in stride. Dad was proud that I had passed my physical, that I was willing to serve our country just as he had.

He didn't realize I knew that he walked out into the backyard and cried.

As it turned out, it was all for naught.

Two weeks passed, then three, then six, and finally I decided to go on with my life and my plans.

I enrolled in Odessa College. I continued to work out too. I got a part-time job at the Inn of the Golden West in Odessa. It was a great job because I was able to eat free and also had plenty of time to do my studies. It was the tallest building in Odessa at that time, all of eleven stories, and it was a perfect place for me to run stairs. I must have made a hundred trips up and down those stairs over the next few months. Between the lifting and the stairs, I was in great shape.

It was two years later when I ran into a guy who worked for the Selective Service. I explained to him what had happened regarding my draft experience. He asked me if I changed my address or if I was ever reclassified. I told him that I had not moved and I hadn't heard anything else from them since the physical. He said, "If you passed your physical in 1968 and did not receive your induction notice or any further notification, then your folder must have somehow been put in a wrong file."

He also said, "God must have been watching out for you."

Looking back, I know that is exactly what happened. Had I gone to Vietnam at that point in my life, I probably wouldn't have lasted six weeks before I'd have been hurt, if not killed.

———————

Somehow word got around to the coaches at Sul Ross that I was back in Odessa and no longer involved with football. It had been three years since the Sul Ross coaches had watched me play, but they were still interested. Frank Krhut, the defensive coordinator for Sul Ross, called me at home and said he would be in Odessa in a few days. He wanted to meet.

I was excited about the possibility of getting another shot at football. Sul Ross was a member of the Lone Star Conference, which had received more and more attention on a national scale because of the number of great athletes it was producing each year. I had been hesitant when the Lobos offered me a full scholarship back in 1966, but now I was hungry and wanted to play again. I wasn't going to mention it to Coach Krhut, but I was ready to walk on and play without a scholarship.

As it turned out, that wasn't the plan.

The minute Coach Krhut walked into the restaurant at the Inn of the Golden West, he sized me up and down. We shook hands, and he said, "You look like a linebacker." The last time Coach had seen me, I weighed around 150 pounds. Now I was about 185 pounds and I was twenty years old. Coach got right to the bottom line. He said, "Mike, we can give you a full scholarship if you want to come play football at Sul Ross; we need a good defensive back, and I think you can be that guy."

I tried not to show my excitement, but I was doing backflips on the inside. "Okay, I'd love to. I can't wait to get started."

We talked for a few minutes about the program, the conference, and the school. Coach Krhut did his best recruiting job, but I had been sold when he called me on the phone.

I was ready to start playing football again, and Sul Ross seemed like the perfect place for me to make a comeback and play my final three years.

FIVE DAD HAD THREE RULES

Dad showed his love for me by the amount of time we spent together. He'd load me and our dogs in the family station wagon, and we would go fishing on the Pecos River south of Odessa. In later years my younger sister, Pam, joined us. She was a tomboy and always wanted to be just like me. For several years, though, it was just Dad and me.

It was on these trips to the river, amid the isolation it afforded, that we sat by the campfire and talked. The stories he told me about his past and the things he had done had an amazing impact on my life. Those stories affected many of the split-second decisions I made for many years to come.

It was on the trips to the river where I first learned about the mind games. Dad didn't call them mind games; that was a name I gave them as I got older. He just called it "being ready" to protect myself.

When I was six years old, Dad decided it was time for me to learn how to box. He handed me a new pair of gloves, showed me how to pull them on with my teeth, and then laced them up for me. He pulled his gloves on, got down on his knees, and we started a routine that went on for almost seven years in the living room of our home.

I learned how to set my feet and how to throw punches without leaving myself wide open. I learned how to throw combinations and hit equally well with my right and my left. He taught me how to use my feet for defense and offense, and I learned how to take a punch.

Dad popped me pretty good sometimes, and my nose would bleed. Or he'd bust my lips. As badly as I wanted to cry, I could not. It wasn't an option.

He told me I had to be tough; I had to be quick. He reminded me that I was small, and that bigger kids would bully me if I didn't learn how to fight.

Sometimes Mom argued with him about hitting me too hard. But he would hug me and tell Mom I was okay. He told me I was tough and I could handle it. And he was right—I could. I never had a fear of being hit by other kids—older, bigger, or stronger. I knew they would never hit me as hard as my dad did.

I guess I was about thirteen when Dad and I boxed for the last time. It was a Saturday, and he was boxing with me and trying to watch the baseball game of the week on television at the same time. He had his hands up to protect himself but kept turning his head to see the game. I'd been boxing with him for almost seven years, and I was pretty good at it by now. I planted my feet and threw a right cross with everything I had, right between his raised hands, and caught him flush in the side of the face.

Down he went.

I don't know which one of us was more shocked. I couldn't believe it, and I don't think he could either.

Dad sat back up, shook off his gloves, smiled at me, and said, "Okay, you are too big to box with me on my knees, and you're not big enough to box with standing up, so we're not boxing anymore."

Then he laid down the law—his law.

"But there is something I want to tell you, and I don't want you to forget this. If I ever hear of you starting a fight, you're going to get a whippin' when you get home. If I ever hear of someone starting a fight with you and you don't fight back, you're getting a whippin' when you get home. If I hear of you fighting and you don't win, you're getting a whippin' when you get home."

We never boxed again after that day, and I don't think he ever reminded me again of his "three rules."

But I remembered every word.

———

I was about ten years old when I first saw my dad get in a fight. There was a turkey shoot at the local American Legion, and he was one of the judges.

Targets had been set up inside metal containers, and the men had a shooting contest using .22-caliber rifles. The winner won a smoked turkey. There were drinks and food, and it was a lot of fun being there with my dad.

These guys were good shots.

Two of the contestants had both hit the bull's-eye, eliminating everyone else. The shots were so close to center that it was hard to tell which shot was the best. Dad picked up two brass shell casings and pushed one of them through each of the holes in the targets. The brass gave a better definition of the hole, and it was easier to see which hole was closer to center. Dad looked at the targets and said, "These are both such great shots, I hate to pick a winner and a loser."

One of the guys said, "I think he's got me beat."

Dad said, "Well, I am glad you said that; I think he does too. It looks real close, but I think his is a bit closer to center than your shot."

Well, there was another guy there, a big ol' guy who had watched the contest and stood behind my dad as he checked the targets. You could tell this guy had been drinking. He pushed my father on the shoulder and asked, "Who authorized you to say this guy wins and this guy loses?"

Dad turned around and faced him. "I've been appointed the official judge of this contest."

The guy said, "But why? This guy's a veteran and this guy's a veteran, so now you're saying he wins, and he loses?"

The man in the contest who had conceded the prize said to this guy, "Hey, look. His shot is a truer shot than mine. He has won the turkey."

But the big guy didn't stop. He pointed to my dad and said, "I just want to know what qualifies this guy to make the decision." Dad turned around and looked straight at me and said, "I want you to leave." As soon as the other men around my dad heard that, they stepped between him and the big guy and immediately said to the guy, "We want you to leave. Please leave right now."

I was young, but I had a good idea of what was going on. I knew my dad, and I was scared. In response to the man's question about Dad's qualifications as a judge at this veteran's event, Dad said, "I am an American. I have slept in as many foxholes as any man here and been shot at by as many Germans, and I am an American."

As soon as Dad made the statement, the man looked at him and said, "You ain't no American."

That's the last thing the guy said at the turkey shoot.

My dad was furious. He floored him with one punch. I knew Dad was strong and had an unbelievable grip, and that was one reason he could hit so hard. I had seen him take an apple and slowly turn it to mush as he squeezed it in his hand. And I knew that's what this guy's head would have looked like if the other men hadn't pulled Dad off the guy.

That was a side of Dad that I had never seen before, but it was consistent with the stories he told me about himself on our trips to the river.

As I got older I realized that the boxing lessons with my dad went way beyond just throwing punches and defending myself. They extended to the vivid stories he told me—the things we discussed while we fished, or relaxed on the patio of our home, or rested in the living room after we boxed. Dad was trying to teach me how to be mentally ready at all times, and I took it to the next level and began to play "mind games." They would be both a blessing and a curse as I grew from a child into a teenager and a young adult.

Dad told me things that might sound bizarre to other people but made a lot of sense to me. He said, "Mike, if you are sitting down and somebody is standing over you, I don't care what they say to you; you just sit there and don't say anything. Wait until they turn and walk away and you can get on your feet. Then, once you're on your feet, you can take care of business.

"Never sit on the inside of the booth. Always sit where you can get up. If you're with other people, let them have the inside seats; you sit on the outside.

"If you are in the car, you make sure you have time to get out before someone can get to you, and then you state your piece. If you are somewhere and know you're going to fight—and believe me, you'll know—fight right then and there. Don't go outside. Don't give them a chance to get some buddies to help them. Don't give them time to pick up something they can hit you with.

"When you knock someone down, never get on them. They can grab you and pull a knife out of their pocket. When you knock them down, stomp or kick them; don't let them get back up."

No matter where I was, be it in the neighborhood, at school, in a bar or in a restaurant, I always watched other people. Most of the time I sensed potential troublemakers. By watching people and how they acted, I could usually tell who was going to cause problems.

I immediately started to visualize an altercation with them in my mind. I went through different scenarios, but every time, I won the mental fight. I was amazed by how many fights actually happened because I expected them to happen.

In most of these situations normal people would look at what was happening and say to themselves, *Those guys are looking for trouble; I think I'll just go somewhere else.* My thoughts would be, *Those guys are looking for trouble. I'll hang around and see what happens.*

I venture to guess that, outside of television and the movies, most people can go their entire lives and never witness a fistfight, much less get involved in one. But not only did I not mind fighting, I was good at it. That created a lot of opportunities for me, because there was always somebody in West Texas who knew me, had heard about me, or just didn't care—they just wanted to fight.

That is just how it was in West Texas.

I was involved in more than thirty fights over a three-year span from 1968 through 1971. I was arrested five times and busted my right hand at least six times.

When I was arrested for fighting, I'd call Dad and he'd bail me out of jail. He would act angry about it at the time.

But I knew he wasn't really upset with me.

My memories of my dad weren't only about boxing. I probably laughed more at my dad than anyone else in my life. He had a great sense of humor and loved practical jokes, even when he was the brunt of the joke.

Once when I was around twelve years old, I hid in the bathroom of our home for almost an hour and waited for him to come to bed. He was up watching the news and he thought I had gone to bed long ago. I stood in the bathtub, behind the shower curtain, with my hand over the light switch. When Dad finally walked down the hall and reached his hand around the inside of the door to turn on the bathroom light, he grabbed my hand instead of the light switch.

I squeezed his hand, and he almost jerked me out of the tub as he jumped back. He knew after a second it was me, but the initial shock of expecting to flip on a light and being grabbed by a warm hand really shocked him. He laughed about being scared by my stunt and sent me to bed. I fell asleep with a grin on my face. It was so much fun scaring Dad.

Another priceless memory I have of my dad happened one weekend when I was in high school. Dad and I were fishing at our favorite spot on the Pecos River. We had a small aluminum boat that we rowed up and down the river to places where the banks were too rugged or steep for us to walk.

We had fished downriver early one morning and were paddling our way back to camp against the current. The current was pretty stiff, and as I looked down through the water, I saw it was only a few feet deep at that spot. Dad was up in the front of the boat working feverishly, so I told him just to stop and rest. I slid over the side of the boat into the water and started walking behind the boat in an attempt to push us the rest of the way to shore.

Dad was sitting in the front of the boat with the oar across his lap, enjoying the ride and the rest from all the hard paddling. I was in water about four feet deep walking behind the little aluminum boat, inching it toward shore. I looked around the boat and noticed we were only about ten feet from shore. Without saying anything to Dad, I just decided to give the boat one big push to get it to the riverbank.

I shoved the boat as hard as I could, and Dad tumbled backward. From my vantage point in the water, all I saw were his feet sticking straight up in the air as he landed on his back between the benches in the boat. That wasn't the biggest problem we had to deal with, though. I didn't shove the boat hard enough to get it to shore.

I stood helpless in the water and watched as the current caught the boat, turned it back downstream, and took the boat. Dad, with his glasses hanging on by one ear and his hat sideways, cussed and struggled to get upright.

I nearly drowned because I was laughing so hard.

Dad righted himself, turned the boat around, and started to paddle back to shore against the current. At first he was mad because he had floated right into an area where some other men were fishing. When they'd walked by us earlier, he had instructed them to not get too close to where we were fishing. But then he started to laugh just as loud as I did, and he admitted it must have looked pretty funny. It was hilarious, but he also told me that was the last time he would ever let me push him anywhere in a boat.

After I met with Coach Krhut in the fall of 1968, we agreed that I would start classes at Sul Ross in January 1969. This would give me an opportunity to meet the team, go through the off-season program, and be ready for the 1969 season.

While I trained at a gym in Odessa in preparation for the football season, I met a guy named Sam Sizemore, who was four years older than I was. I had known of Sam because we lived in the same neighborhood, but due to our age difference, he didn't know me. We struck up a friendship and trained together. Sam told me he was headed to Sul Ross to finish his degree, and I told him I was headed there to play football. Since I had recently totaled my car, Sam agreed to give me a ride to Alpine.

Things seemed to be falling into place.

We left that January for Alpine. Sam filled me in on the Lone Star Conference along the way. He talked about Sul Ross and its football program, and then he made a prediction: "Sul Ross has a good football team, and they will probably do well this year, but there is one team you guys are never going to beat, and that's Texas A&I. They play Southwest Conference football." I just tucked that bit of information away in my memory.

I was at Sul Ross for less than a week when I ended up in the city jail for—you guessed it—fighting. It was before we started spring practices in football. A bunch of players went to a party one night just outside of Alpine in the small city of Marathon. We had too many "Sneaky Pete" drinks—a wine and beer concoction—before we headed back into town.

We were pretty drunk, one thing led to another, and I got into a fight with some cowboys. During the altercation I kicked out a window at the Methodist Church Student Center. I don't remember why I happened to be there, but it certainly wasn't to pray. When the fight ended I jumped back into the car and went to my off-campus dormitory and to bed.

The Alpine police showed up later that night and knocked on my door. I had no idea what was going on, and it didn't register to me that the guys at my door were policemen. Not even their uniforms, badges, and holstered guns were clear enough hints, because I was still wasted from those Sneaky Pete drinks. They told me to get dressed and come with them.

When I first arrived at the police station, I still had no clue what was happening. It wasn't until four policemen led me into a cell that I realized I was in jail. I knew this wasn't good. My mind started to race. My next thought was, *I have to get out of here right now.*

One of the policemen had a can of mace, and he was the first one I punched. When he landed on the floor, he started spraying me with mace and it blinded me. I didn't know which way was out, but as a fighter I knew what to expect next. I knew I didn't have any friends in that jail, so I kicked and punched anyone who came close to me. All I saw were blurry images, because my eyes burned and watered from the mace.

One of the policemen hit me across the top of the head with his pistol and knocked me down. I immediately scrambled to my feet, but he knocked me down again with another blow from his pistol. When he hit me that second time, I knew I had to stay down and protect myself. This wasn't a good position to be in, and I knew what was coming next. I rolled up into a ball as tightly as I could and tried to cover my head while these policemen stomped and kicked the living daylights out of me.

When they finally stopped beating on me, they dragged me to a cell and left me. I eventually got to my feet and wouldn't stay quiet. I repeatedly screamed, "You've got to let me make a phone call!" The police told me I needed to shut up because there were mourners across the street at the funeral home. Finally, the police let me make my telephone call, and I dialed Sul Ross assistant football coach Al Parsons.

I said, "Coach, I am over here in jail."

Coach Parsons said, "Mike, we know you are in jail, and we're working on it."

A highway patrolman had walked into the police station as I made my telephone call to Coach Parsons. I had taken off my shirt and was holding it on top of my head to stop the bleeding from the gashes where the policeman had pistol-whipped me. The highway patrolman looked at me and asked one of the police officers, "What is going on?" The officer answered, "This guy has been causing trouble, and we've allowed him to call his coaches." The patrolman said, "This kid is losing a lot of blood; you've got to get him some medical attention. What were you thinking?"

The police took me to the emergency room, where a doctor cleaned and stitched my head wounds. They hauled me back to jail, and the next morning I was in court. Four eyewitnesses who saw my fight with the cowboys were in the courtroom, as well as a few of my football coaches and the four arresting police officers.

I must have looked pretty scary. My T-shirt was caked in dried blood. My partially shaved head, full of stitches, was red, swollen, and covered with dark, dried blood. My nose was three times its normal size, my eyes were black, almost swollen shut, and my teeth were stained with blood from the cuts on my lips and mouth. A female judge sat looking at me for a minute, then read the charges against me and asked, "Mr. Flynt, how do you plead?"

I said, "Your Honor, I have no idea. I may have done everything you just read; I don't know. I honestly don't remember. I was drunk, and I don't know whether I did those things or not."

The judge said, "Well, then you plead *nolo contendere*. That means you don't admit to the charges and you don't deny them; you just let the facts speak for themselves."

I said, "Okay, ma'am, then that's how I plead."

She then said, "Mr. Flynt, let me ask you a question. If you didn't do all the things you've been accused of, if you weren't fighting and didn't kick out that glass window, then how do you account for the blood all over you and the way you look?"

I had hoped she would ask.

I turned and pointed at the four arresting police officers and said, "Well, Your Honor, these four officers were putting me in jail last night; I was drunk and resisted, and this officer on the end here felt like it was necessary to pistol-whip me. Then the other officers stomped me and kicked me after I was down. That's how I account for how I look, the blood all over me, and these stitches in the top of my head."

The judge turned and stared at the officers and didn't say a word for several seconds, and then she said, "Okay, I need to hear from the witnesses."

I think these witnesses were all pretty shocked by my condition because the first guy called to the stand said, "I saw the guy who got in the fight last night. I mean, I was there. But he didn't look anything like this guy. I can't say for sure if it was this guy or not. If that's him, I don't recognize him."

The next three guys said the same thing. The judge pounded her gavel and said, "Case dismissed. Mr. Flynt, you are free to go." Then she looked at the four arresting police officers and told them she wanted to talk to them in her chambers immediately.

I didn't stick around to hear the outcome of that conversation. I was more worried about the coaches at this point than anything else. Coach Jerry Larned, one of my defensive coaches, was present. His primary concern was how long it would be before I could wear a helmet again. I healed quickly; I'd had a lot of practice at that too.

———————

I'd be a liar if I said I wasn't comfortable with who I was. I admit I took fighting beyond my dad's instructions and I stretched his rules. You can call it ego, ignorance, self-righteousness, or just the foolishness of my youth, but I felt good about the man I was, and I had a lot of confidence in what I could do.

Late one night Randy Wilson, Roel Maldonado, Glen McWhorter, and I decided to go to the truck stop on the edge of town in Alpine to eat. Randy and I had been involved in a fight at this same truck stop three weeks earlier, but we had taken it outside and there was no property damage. We didn't feel like it would be a problem for us to go back. We were lucky that time. The police were called, but we took off and they didn't show up at our dormitory.

The first thing I did when I walked through the door this time was look around to see who was there and quickly try to determine what person or persons might be a potential source of trouble. The only red flag was the guy who worked behind the counter. He was a part-time manager and a cook. He was a tall, lanky guy, about six foot three, 195 pounds, and probably around forty years old.

As he looked at us, he reached under the counter and picked up a wide-mouth jar. There was something in that jar. I couldn't tell what it was, but it was the way he looked at us that had me concerned. We piled into a booth. I took my place on the outside, and a waitress took our order.

Randy, who played defensive end for us, pulled up a wooden chair and parked his six-foot-two, 250-pound body at the end of the booth. As he leaned back in the chair, he got this strange look on his face because the legs on the chair had started to give way and crack. Well, the chair collapsed, and Randy fell flat on his rear on top of the broken chair. We all started to laugh because everyone thought it was pretty darn funny.

The guy behind the counter didn't laugh.

As he made his way to our booth, I noticed he had his right hand under his apron. He grabbed the back of Randy's shirt as he was getting another chair and said, "Come on. You're coming with me." I said, "Wait a minute. What are you talking about? Going with you where?" He answered, "He's going to jail." I said, "Hold on a minute. Look, we'll pay you for the chair. We don't want any trouble. We'll pay you for the chair and our food and we'll leave."

He said again, "No, he's going to jail."

Then the guy pulled his hand from underneath the apron, and I finally saw what he was hiding. It was a blackjack, a small club with a lead weight about the size of a golf ball sewn in between two thick pieces of leather. It also has a leather strap to put your hand through so you can secure it to your wrist.

He showed me the blackjack and started flipping it in his hand like he had used it before. He then surprised me because he knew my name. He said, "Flynt, he's going to jail, and if you try to stop me, I'm going to use this slapper on him."

I said, "I'll tell you what. He's not going anywhere with you, and if you try to hit him with that slapper, I'll take it away from you and make you eat it."

He accepted the challenge.

In one motion he turned Randy loose, squared up with me, and said, "Why don't you do that?" And so I thought, *You got it.*

As I stepped toward him, he swung at me with the blackjack. I threw up my left arm to block the blow, but I was only partially successful. He caught me with a glancing blow, just behind my left ear. It was hard enough that I saw stars. I knew I didn't want to let him hit me with it again. As I blocked his swing with my left arm, I reached back with my right and caught him in the face with a right cross. He went down.

Now this may sound strange to most people, but normally when you fight with someone on the spur of the moment, it's not a personal thing. It's either self-defense or a difference of opinion you choose to settle physically, or it has something to do with alcohol—or maybe all of the above. But when it is personal, then there's an almost uncontrollable rage that takes over, and that's usually when people get hurt.

When he threatened to use that blackjack on Randy, he made it personal with me.

I stepped over this guy and held the blackjack in my left hand and hit him with my right. I hit him again and again as I tried to pull the blackjack off his wrist. I'd made up my mind that I wanted to rip that blackjack away from him and shove it in his mouth, just like I promised. As I continued to yank at the blackjack, I noticed the look of panic in his eyes. He knew exactly what I was going to do if I got my hands on it, and he was doing everything in his power to keep that from happening.

I actually pulled him to his feet as I tried to get the blackjack off his wrist.

As we struggled across the restaurant, we overturned tables and broke coffee cups, glasses, and everything in our path. The counter bar was half the length of the restaurant. A glass display case filled with pies was on top of the bar. We wrestled into the bar and knocked the display case onto the floor. An assortment of pies splattered all over the floor.

The struggle now was totally over the blackjack. I was on a mission, and my focus was to get that weapon and give this guy what he'd intended to give Randy.

I didn't see it, but I felt the impact and heard the moan from this guy as Randy brought a wooden chair across the dude's back with a full swing. The splintered wood flew. For a moment our opponent just went limp and started to fall. But I had hold of the blackjack, and that kept him upright.

I turned to where I could see Randy. He had another chair. He raised it to arm's length straight up overhead and knocked out all the fluorescent lights in the process. I stepped back and turned the guy loose. Randy brought that chair down across the guy's head and shoulders. Blood and pieces of wood flew everywhere.

And just that quickly, it was over.

This guy was out cold on the floor, covered in blood. The whole restaurant was a wreck. Customers stood with their mouths open, frozen as they'd watched the fight. I looked at Randy and said, "I think we'd better get out of here." I wasn't worried about the blackjack anymore; I was worried about the police.

We took off, but the police caught up with us, and we were in court the next morning. The guy from the truck stop showed, and his head was one big gauze bandage. All I could see were his eyes and a little bit of hair that stuck straight up out of the bandages wrapped around his head. He had a broken collarbone, and his arm was in a sling. We told our side of the story and this guy told his. The judge apparently liked our story better, because he just fined us one hundred dollars each and let us go.

As we left the courthouse, one of the deputy sherriffs told me this guy had beaten up a couple of college students pretty badly with that blackjack. He said the judge knew about that, and he was certain it'd had some bearing on our case. We were told later that Sherriff Skinner had arrived at the scene and laughed, telling the guy with the blackjack, "Looks like you messed with the wrong guys this time!"

After that fight the Sul Ross administration declared the truck stop off-limits for college students. I had made the dean's list—and it was not the good list. The coaches warned me to stay out of trouble, but trouble stayed with me 24-7.

A few of my teammates—Bob Hayter, Smokey Eppler, and Stan Williamson—were genuine cowboys. They were a tough group. These guys worked on ranches and felt as comfortable on a horse as off. These were the first real cowboys I had ever been around. Not only could they ride and rope, they were good football players too.

Smokey always talked about country-and-western dancing and how much fun it was. He talked about the cute girls who wore tight Wrangler jeans and how they loved to dance close and do the two-step. Smokey didn't have to sell me.

I loved to dance and loved to meet nice-looking girls. My first country-and-western dance was held in the Sul Ross gymnasium. I had quite a few friends there that night, but I noticed a bunch of cute girls near the bottom row of the bleachers. I figured that would be as good a place as any for me to find a seat.

The dance was being held in the basketball arena, and the bleachers were only partially pulled out, so there was plenty of room for dancing. A band played at the far end of the gym on a stage, and tables were set up on the floor. There weren't many tables, however, and most of the students were either dancing or just standing around talking. Sul Ross is a rodeo college, and students loved their country-and-western dancing. It was crowded, and everyone was having a good time.

I sat down in an open spot on the bottom row of the bleachers, right in the middle of about five girls. Between the band and the crowd it was pretty noisy, so everyone was seated on the bleachers in small groups where we could hear each other talk.

I introduced myself as I sat down next to a girl named Paige, and we started playing the "do you know" game. All of a sudden a big cowboy walked up, grabbed Paige by the arm, and said, "Let's go dance." She gave me a strange look and got up, and they headed for the dance floor.

The cowboy brought her back a few minutes later, but Paige was real quiet. I didn't think anything about it at the time; I was busy talking to the other girls. The cowboy returned a few minutes later, and they went out and danced again. During a pause in my conversation with one of the other girls, I noticed that Paige had sat back down. The lighting wasn't that great, but I could tell she was upset. I leaned toward her and saw tears streaming down her face.

"Hey, what's up with you?"

She looked down, shook her head, and said, "I'm scared."

I said, "Scared? Of what?"

She pointed at the cowboy approaching and said, "Him! I'm scared of him."

I asked, "Isn't that your boyfriend?"

She answered, "I have no idea who he is. I've never seen him before."

"You are kidding me!" I said. She just shook her head.

I asked her, "You don't want to dance with this guy?"

She said, "No, but he won't leave me alone."

I said, "Yeah, he will."

When the cowboy walked back up and reached for Paige again, I reached out and grabbed his arm and said, "She doesn't want to dance."

He glared at me and said, "Well, how about you, do you want to dance?"

I said, "You're darn right I do."

"Well, let's go outside," he said.

I told him there were too many cops outside and I didn't want anyone breaking this up, but the men's bathroom was empty. I was furious with this guy for what he had done to Paige. He was a challenge—I could tell he had fought before—but I finally got the best of him. He said he had had enough, asked me to stop, and so I let it go.

I told him, "I am leaving now because the cops will be back here in a minute. You'd better not say another word to that girl." He shook his head no, he would not.

I found out later that this cowboy was a football recruit on his initial visit to Sul Ross. Coach Harvey telephoned me the next morning and said, "We've got a recruit in here who got the daylights beat out of him last night. Do you know anything about that?"

I said, "No, sir, I do not."

I am not sure Coach Harvey believed me, but he said, "Okay" and hung up.

Ten years later, as the strength and conditioning coach at Texas A&M, I hosted a clinic for Texas high school coaches. One of the coaches approached me, introduced himself, and asked me if I remembered him. I looked at him with my mind racing, hoping for a memory, but told him I did not. He said, "You beat the crap out of me one night at a dance in Alpine." Then it immediately came back to me. He said, "I had that coming, and I got exactly what I deserved." He went on to say, "That night was the last time I had any alcohol to drink."

Finals were over in the fall semester of 1969, and I headed home to Odessa. I usually worked in the oil fields as a roughneck because the money was good and they knew this was a part-time gig for me.

I worked right up until December 31 without a day off, and I looked forward to a night on the town on New Year's Eve. It started out to be a pretty boring evening. I celebrated the new year and then went home and went to bed.

Around one thirty in the morning, Randy Wilson came in my house (my parents never locked the door). He woke me up and said he and Mike Arnold (Stubby) had just arrived from Midland and wanted me to get up and go party with them. Midland is where Randy lived and is located about twenty miles from Odessa. I reluctantly got up and got dressed, and we went back out on the town. We wound up at the Inn of the Golden West, where I had previously worked.

There were several all-night parties at the Inn, and we went from floor to floor, party to party. Then I remembered Jackson. I wondered if he was working late cleaning up after all the parties.

When I had worked at the Inn of the Golden West the previous year, I had met a guy who was a few years older than I was chronologically. But because of brain damage as a baby, he was mentally like a nine- or ten-year-old kid. When the cook had introduced us, he had introduced him to me as "Jack." But when we shook hands, he told me his name was "Jackson." That's what I always called him.

Jackson was a hard worker, about five foot eight and weighed about 165 pounds. He was always happy. He really liked me because I was the only college football player he knew, and the cook used to tell me I was Jackson's hero. I always tried to stop and say hello to Jackson before I started work.

I knew if Jackson was there on New Year's Eve he would be in the private restaurant on the top floor. I told Randy and Stubby I wanted to see if Jackson was working, so we jumped on the elevator and headed up to the eleventh floor.

Lo and behold, when the elevator doors opened, there was Jackson. He was covered in sweat as he lugged a huge rubber trash can full of empty and half-empty bottles and other party-related trash. He didn't see me until we got off the elevator and I called his name. I exclaimed, "Jackson, happy New Year!"

The little boy in the man was so excited he practically ran over to me and accidentally bumped some of the patrons as they left the restaurant. Unfortunately, one of them was a manager, and she had been overserved from the bar.

Jackson tried to apologize, but he wouldn't look at his manager. He kept his eyes on me, and I could tell he was scared. She threw a fit and began to cuss him and belittle him in front of several people as they waited to get on one of the two elevators.

I stepped in and tried to explain what had happened, but she wouldn't let me get a word in edgewise. Jackson leaned over and asked me to not say anything to her because he was afraid she would fire him. I told him I wouldn't say a word.

We stood there and listened to her insult him, and then she looked at me and told me to leave and not interfere with his work. I didn't respond; I just glared at her. The elevator doors opened, and she, her husband, and their crowd got on the elevator and scowled at us as the doors closed.

I introduced Jackson to Randy and Stubby. When I told him that Stubby was a rodeo clown and what dangerous work that was, Jackson had a new hero. We had a good visit, and then Jackson had to get back to work. I could tell he was pretty shaken; we needed to leave.

We got back in the elevator and headed to the lobby. The doors opened, and there stood the rude manager with her husband and a crowd of people from one of the parties upstairs. We had no choice but to walk through them as we got off the elevator. I hoped she wouldn't say anything to me, but it didn't happen that way.

She popped off and I responded. I'd had time to think about all she had said to Jackson as I rode down in the elevator. When I walked out of the elevator, it was not a good thing that she was there.

When I returned her verbal abuse, her husband pushed his way through the crowd and moved toward me. I heard Randy behind me say, "I've got him." The guy never saw Randy. To this day I know he thinks one of the elevators fell on him. Randy "dough-popped" this guy, and the first thing that hit the wall was his head. The fight was on. Total mayhem broke out as the slugfest ensued.

It quickly spilled outside, which was to our advantage because their group had us outnumbered by at least three to one. Some guy drove his car right up to where the fight was, hit his brakes, jumped out, rolled up his sleeves, and said, "I think I'll get me a little bit of this."

I hit him right between the eyes.

He was still laid out in the parking lot when we left in the police car. I think he got a little bit more than he wanted.

The police arrived en masse. They grabbed everyone, put us in handcuffs and stuck us in police cars—everyone except for Randy. When the cops started to arrive, Randy just casually walked away.

Stubby was in the backseat of the squad car. I was handcuffed and in the front on the passenger side. The cop put me in the car and slammed the door but left the window down. While he took statements from other people, the female manager who had jumped all over Jackson walked up to the car on my side, husband in tow.

Her husband cussed me and told me what he would do to me if I wasn't in the police car. She then cussed me and spit in my face through the window. They both turned and began to walk away.

My hands were cuffed behind my back, but I twisted around and flipped the handle on the door, shoved the door open, and stepped out of the car. The look on that guy's face when he saw me was priceless.

With my hands cuffed, I wasn't about to give him a chance. I kicked him in the chest, and he fell back against a parked car. I then kicked him in the groin, and he went down. Before the police got to me, I landed three or four more well-placed kicks.

Two policemen grabbed me, one on each side. As they led me back to the car, we walked right past the woman who had spit on me. I returned the favor when I got directly in front of her. For the first time all night, she didn't say a word. She just glared at me, and then she looked away.

Stubby and I went to jail that night. We made bail the next day and were released. I had to be back at school in less than two weeks, so I just kept roughnecking right up until the time I had to leave for Alpine.

I stopped by to see Jackson at the Inn of the Golden West before I left. He was doing great. He told me nothing else was ever said to him about the misunderstanding on New Year's Eve. I didn't tell him about anything else that had happened that night. I was just glad to be going back to school.

That's the last time I ever saw my friend Jackson.

SIX THE STRAW THAT BROKE THE CAMEL'S BACK

Alpine, a small city of about six thousand people, is snuggled against the Davis Mountains in the Big Bend Country of southwestern Texas. It has been described as the last great frontier and is as remote as a medieval castle.

Back in the Old West, Alpine was a stop along the transcontinental Southern Pacific Railroad. The final segment of the railroad began in two directions in 1881. One segment was built eastward from El Paso and reached Alpine in April 1882, while the other segment was built westward from San Antonio. The last spike connecting the rails was driven near Langtry on January 12, 1883.

Alpine is known for its unique charm because of its friendly people, mild climate, and breathtaking mountain setting. But, unique charm or not, it felt like you were in the middle of nowhere as a college student there.

Sul Ross State, meanwhile, was named for former Texas governor, Civil War hero, and patriot, Lawrence Sullivan Ross. It was founded in 1917 as Sul Ross Normal College and was made a full university when I arrived in 1969. It had about two thousand students, and teacher education was one of its most popular programs.

The football team faced a number of unique problems because of Alpine's isolation.

The nearest community is either Fort Davis, location of the world-renowned McDonald Observatory, or Marfa, an art community and home of the mysterious "Marfa lights." Both are about 26 miles away. The nearest city of fifty thousand is Odessa, 160 miles to the northeast. Richard Harvey, our head football coach at Sul Ross, explained it perfectly when he said in a newspaper interview, "You've almost got to be going to Alpine to come here."

Coach Harvey was in his second year at Sul Ross in 1969. He was a former All-Conference quarterback at North Texas State. Coach Krhut was the staff's grizzled veteran, so to speak, because he was in his eighth season at the college. Assistant coaches Al Parsons and Jerry Larned were each in their second season.

While Coach Harvey concentrated his recruiting efforts on the Permian Basin area of Texas and New Mexico, he had to look much farther for games. He was forced to travel to cities such as Portales, New Mexico, three hundred miles away, to find nonconference opponents and to cities such as San Marcos, about five hundred miles away, to find Lone Star Conference opponents.

Our closest competitor was Angelo State University, and San Angelo was more than two hundred miles away. Coach Harvey figured we'd have to travel more than six thousand miles a year to play five road games.

While recruiting also proved to be a challenge for Harvey due to time and distance, he believed the staff had a great chance to sign players when they visited the campus. "There is a certain attraction to Alpine and to Sul Ross. It is a new world to people from the big cities and one that most of them really like."

Harvey believed another factor that made us successful was the bond we formed because of our isolation from other schools and cities. "The isolation, the distance from here to anyplace else, instills a camaraderie among our players that we feel is a good thing. Then, add to this the fact we go into almost every game we play as the underdog, and it really pulls our kids together. We are backed into a corner before we begin, and we have to come out fighting."

I could relate.

We ended our 1970 season with an upset win over heavily favored Angelo State, 27-14, in late November. In fact, the local newspaper reported the following day that Sul Ross State "bounced the Angelo State Rams around San Angelo Stadium."

The story continued: "Coach Richard Harvey's Lobos came to San Angelo with a purpose and went about the job of obtaining their goals as they sliced big holes in the highly regarded ASU defense and played some fine defense of their own."

It was all true, as we outgained the Rams by more than a hundred yards and ran an astonishing thirty-four more plays on offense. Our defense forced three turnovers and limited the Rams to just seven points in the second half.

It was also a great win because we snapped the Rams' five-game winning streak and prevented them from finishing with a school-record seven victories on the season. They really wanted to set that mark. We were thrilled because the victory was our seventh overall and we finished the season tied for second place in the Lone Star Conference standings.

We had a good trip back to Alpine. Our season was over, but our thoughts were already on the next year. As we unloaded our equipment back at our locker room, I stepped up on one of the benches and told my teammates the only reason we lost three games that season to Texas A&I, McMurry College, and East Texas State was because we played as a bunch of individuals. But when we played as a team like we did against a two-touchdown-favorite Angelo State team, there wasn't anyone in the country that could beat us. And I meant every word of it. I knew we could win the Lone Star Conference in 1971, and that was my goal.

I had a solid junior year at linebacker. I was named the Lone Star Conference Defensive Player of the Week after our second game against Tarleton State. I was also named Honorable Mention All–Lone Star Conference at weakside linebacker at the end of the season. I was by far the smallest linebacker in the conference at 195 pounds. We actually had eleven players who earned first-team, second-team, or honorable mention status. The only school who had more players recognized as "Lone Star Aces" was the team we beat the last game of the season, Angelo State, and they had thirteen.

At our team banquet in December, I was voted by my teammates as a co-winner of the Most Conscientious Player Award, along with offensive guard Dewayne Richters. I was also named to the Century Club for the second consecutive season with more than one hundred tackles, and to top it off, I was elected one of the team captains for the 1971 season.

I started to prepare for our next season that January while I was at home in Odessa. As soon as I got back to school I trained in a makeshift weight room under the stadium with Erich Hardaway, our All-American shot-putter and discus thrower.

My dad had taught me well in the art of discipline since I was very young. I worked as hard by myself as I did with someone else. Now it was paying off. I made some great strides in my conditioning and my strength. At five foot eleven and 195 pounds, I ran a consistent 4.7 forty-yard dash, and I felt better than I ever had about my strength. But I had a problem. Spring drills were just around the corner, and they were really going to interfere with my current workout routine.

But I had a plan.

I knew that as a team captain, if I went to the coaches and told them I didn't want to participate in the spring training drills, they would definitely balk. But I really didn't think I needed to go through those drills. I felt it would do me more harm than good because of what it would cost me in time lost from my own program. Besides, there was always the chance of getting hurt. So I told the coaches and my teammates I had decided to not return for my senior year—that I wanted to take the remaining few hours I needed to graduate during the summer and get my degree in August. That was my way to avoid spring practice without raising any questions. My teammates knew me better than that, but they went along with my story.

I had scheduled all my classes that spring on Tuesdays and Thursdays so I had time to train on my own while my teammates practiced. I had five days each week with no classes, and I hit it hard. After lifting weights and running in the Davis Mountains all spring, I was actually in much better shape than my teammates were after they finished spring training.

With finals over and school out, we said our good-byes for the summer. I headed to Odessa and the oil fields of West Texas. I had worked for Parker Drilling Company roughnecking during the previous summer and on holidays when I was home from school, but this year I was ready for a change.

A high school friend of mine named Mike Martin introduced me to an opportunity with Johnson's Publishing Company. They provided reverse telephone directories for businesses. They were hiring people to solicit businesses door-to-door and collect information for the directory. Not only was the money pretty good, but they also paid all expenses and they were getting ready to go into Fort Collins, Colorado.

I thought, *Man, this is the ticket. Get out of Odessa for the summer, see the Rockies, and get paid too.* Had we not taken a late-night bicycle ride several weeks after we arrived in Colorado, things would have been great.

We loaded up Mike's car and headed for the Rockies.

We each had an allotment for expenses. Mike and I always tried to find the cheapest lodging available so we could pocket some of our expense money. It turned out that we found an ideal situation at a frat house that was all but vacant for the summer. We moved in and made ourselves at home.

My training in Fort Collins was right on schedule. The altitude, at about a mile high, was actually pretty close to the altitude in Alpine, so my conditioning would be perfect for the start of two-a-days. Some of the fraternity guys who stayed behind for the summer wanted to know all about Sul Ross because I told them we planned to win the Lone Star Conference and advance to the playoffs. We had been in Colorado for several weeks now, and we loved "Rocky Mountain High."

One night we decided to take a late-night bicycle ride down to the square in Fort Collins. Some of the guys who lived at the frat house had told us it would be cool if we wanted to take their ten-speeds and go for a ride. Night or day, it didn't matter. Anytime would not be a problem, but they said the bikes were expensive and if we damaged them it was our responsibility to get them fixed. We agreed.

It was about eleven o'clock at night when we left the fraternity house. There was almost no traffic and the ride to the square was only about a mile long. We discovered when we arrived at the square that it was a popular hangout for the local college kids. The area was totally lit up by streetlights, and quite a few people were there.

I made a couple of trips around the square on my bike and struck up a conversation with some girls parked in a Volkswagen. As I sat on my bike and talked in my sexiest Texas twang, one of the girls pointed behind me and said, "Isn't that your friend?"

I turned around as Mike staggered toward me with a dazed look on his face and blood running out of the corner of his left eye. I saw this big dude behind Mike. He picked up Mike's bike, lifted it over his head, and tossed it into the street. He then planted his feet, put his hands on his hips, and just looked at me with a silly grin on his face. Another guy stood between the big guy and a Mustang convertible. Two guys were in the front of the Mustang, and everyone appeared to be having a good laugh at Mike's expense.

I failed to see the humor.

I stepped off my bike and started toward Mike. Mike Martin was a little guy. He was probably five foot eight and weighed 125 pounds. I asked him what happened. Mike had been drinking, and I thought he had run into the Mustang with his bike and the guys were mad at him.

Mike said, "Flynt, I don't really know what happened, but one of those guys just jacked my jaw as I was riding by them and knocked me off my bike." He then turned and pointed and said, "And then that big guy picked up my bike and threw it out in the road."

I told Mike, "You wait here. I'll be right back."

I started across the road toward the big guy and his buddies. He was shifting his weight from side to side and opening and closing his fists. As I approached him, I realized that I had seen guys like this before. It may have been a different town and a different state, but it was the same guy. He was a bully. No one who had ever been in more than a couple of real fistfights would feel the need to act the way this guy was. He was big and putting off a lot of body language hoping I wouldn't get involved.

He was about to be disappointed. I was not that guy.

I took off. I got faster as I got closer, and I literally kicked his butt as I went by him. I kicked him in the groin and caught him with an uppercut as he leaned forward, and he went down. I knew he wouldn't be getting back up for a few minutes.

The other guy behind the Mustang was the one who I figured had blindsided Mike. When he saw what happened to his buddy, he started running back to the Mustang. I had the angle on him, and running at almost full speed, I hit him with my forearm across the side of his face. The last I saw of him was his feet as they followed the rest of his body through the display window of White's Auto Store. The glass exploded in a million pieces. I threw my arms up to cover my face and felt a "slap" across the upper part of my right arm. The store alarm blared so loudly that it was deafening, but it didn't cover the sound of that Mustang as it cranked up behind me.

I wheeled around just as the convertible started to pull away from the curb. I grabbed the guy on the passenger side by the hair with my left hand and grabbed his face with my right hand. I told the guy behind the wheel, "You better not drive off!" The passenger started screaming, "Don't drive off, don't drive off!"

The driver immediately shut off the car. It was then that I looked down at my arm. Every time my heart would beat, blood poured out of two large, open wounds in my right upper arm.

I knew this was not good.

I turned the dude in the Mustang loose and ran to my bike. I told Mike I had to go back to the frat house and get some help. Mike hollered at me to stop and wait. He said, "You've got to go to the hospital. You're bleeding really bad!" I knew the alarm that sounded in White's Auto would bring the police, and I didn't want to wind up in jail in Colorado. I took off for the fraternity house; I remembered one of the guys staying there had a first-aid kit sitting beside his desk.

It was a longer bicycle ride back to the house than I remembered it being to the square. I went in and woke up the guy with the first-aid kit, asking him to grab some bandages and come into the bathroom and help me because I had cut my arm. He freaked out when he saw my arm: "Man, what happened to you?" Then, before I could answer, he said, "You've got to go to the emergency room! I can't do anything to help you with that. If you don't go soon, I'm afraid you're going to bleed to death!" I agreed, and he gave me a ride to the emergency room.

We walked into the ER, and the police were there talking to the guy who had gone through the store window. He had multiple cuts on his head, and I later learned his jaw was broken on both sides. Although he could not speak clearly, he let the police know as best he could when I walked in that I was the one who had hit him. The police headed my way.

The doctor on duty took one look at my arm and told the police my situation was life threatening, and if they wanted to talk with me, they had to do so while he cleaned and closed the wounds to my arm. The police took my statement as the doctor stitched me up. I had two deep cuts that had to be sewn together on the inside to narrow the wounds enough that they could be stitched closed on the outside.

As soon as the doctor finished with me, the police took me to jail while they tried to sort things out. They also wanted to determine who was going to be held liable for the display window at White's Auto Store. One of the officers came into my cell about four in the morning and said, "You need to get up. We've got to take you back to the emergency room; your stitches have come out."

I looked at my arm and asked him what he was talking about. I told him the stitches looked fine to me. He pointed at all the blood in my bed and said, "Something is wrong—you're still losing a lot of blood." Back at the emergency room they found a third gash in my upper arm that wasn't noticed by the previous doctor because he hadn't removed my short-sleeve shirt when he treated the other two gashes.

Once I was stitched up again, the police officers took me back to the fraternity house instead of to jail. They told me the other guys were known troublemakers. They figured my story was true and released me. They said I would be contacted in a few days about the damages at White's Auto Store and a possible court appearance.

I waited for a couple of days, didn't hear anything, and thought, *Forget this, I'm heading home.* I told Mike to take care of himself, and I jumped on a plane back to Texas. It was time to go back anyway; two-a-day practices were starting on August 23.

Before I reported for two-a-day football practice at Sul Ross for my senior year in 1971, I took time to go over to Bonham Junior High School and watch my first cousin, Terry Flynt, play in a football scrimmage. The head coach at Bonham had been my coach at Hood Junior High School several years before. His name was Coach Joe Swan. He was delighted to see me, although I had to introduce myself; he had no idea who I was. I had been training hard all summer in Colorado, and at five foot eleven, I weighed about 200 pounds and was pretty much solid muscle. My dad could not believe how big I had gotten, and neither could Coach Swan. He told me that when I was at Hood Junior High, he'd wanted to give me a chance to play because I was so tough, but he wouldn't put me in a game because he was afraid I would get hurt since I was so small.

I just stood there and shook my head. So that was it. I never could figure out why he wouldn't let me play back then. But now it was time to head back to Alpine to play.

We were scheduled to open the 1971 regular season in less than a month against New Mexico Highlands in Las Vegas on September 11. I showed up for practice, and the coaches and players were glad I was back but not surprised to see me. I had always planned on coming back, but I didn't think it would be with my arm stitched together like a road map.

It was good to be back with my team again. I had thought about them a lot during the summer and wondered if they had trained as hard as I had. I couldn't participate in any contact drills because of my arm, and our head coach, Richard Harvey, was upset. He said, "Why aren't you in pads?"

I showed him my arm, and he asked, "How on earth did you do that?"

I just shook my head, looked down, and didn't say a word. All Coach Harvey said was, "Flynt . . ." And then he walked away.

The sixties were a turbulent time in America.

Segregation was rampant in the Deep South, and black athletes were prohibited from practicing in college sports in the Southwest Conference until Jerry LeVias broke the color barrier in 1965 when he received a football scholarship to Southern Methodist University in Dallas. That meant some of the best black athletes in Texas and in the South played in the Lone Star Conference.

The Lone Star's two dominant teams, Texas A&I and East Texas State, had a number of players drafted by the NFL and AFL. Offensive lineman Gene Upshaw, for example, was a third-round selection by the Oakland Raiders in the NFL draft out of Texas A&M University–Kingsville in 1967. Mercury Morris, a two-time All-American tailback at West Texas A&M, was a third-round selection by the Miami Dolphins in 1968. Tailback Duane Thomas, of West Texas State, was a first-round selection by the Dallas Cowboys in 1970.

Our junior tailback, Willie Dickson, was a shifty runner who had a great season for us in 1970. He rushed for 1,008 yards, led the conference in scoring with 102 points, and was named first-team All–Lone Star Conference at fullback. Freshman tight end Nolyn McMaryion earned the nickname "Super Freshman" and received second-team All–Lone Star Conference honors. Coach Harvey called McMaryion, a six-foot-one, 230-pounder, "the strongest tight end in the conference."

We had a few days of great practices, and the returning lettermen thought that we had a chance to win the Lone Star Conference. I mean, we had already started to talk about winning it all. Texas A&I had won the NAIA national championship the past two years and the Lone Star Conference title the previous four years. But A&I's head coach, Gil Steinke, mentioned Sul Ross as a team to watch in 1971.

We were loaded with speed. We had players who could run at every position. We returned sixteen starters and thirty-one lettermen. Six of our nine returning starters on offense were on the line, which was great news for our running game and Willie Dickson. We also had a high school All-American from Sonora, Texas, Ed Lee Renfro, who had transferred to Sul Ross from Texas Tech. We expected him to be a big help in our offensive scheme. "More size and more depth than at anytime since I've been here," Coach Harvey said in a preseason interview.

Two-a-days were in full swing. Most of the players were just starting to get over the soreness and settling into a routine. Our off-campus dorm, Fletcher Hall, was horseshoe shaped and three stories high. The freshmen were given the third floor and the upperclassmen shared the lower two floors.

Part of the discipline in our preparation for a championship season was being in on time at curfew. Coach Harvey said it was my responsibility as a senior captain to make sure everyone was in their rooms on time.

In the two years I had been at Sul Ross I never had problems or real disagreements on or off the field with any of my teammates. (Our quarterback, Ronnie Bell, and I had swapped licks down on the river once, but that was alcohol related and we both felt bad about it the next day. We shook hands and it was forgotten.) But a freshman named George Henry changed that one evening during two-a-day practices.

George was an incoming freshman. His older brother had played at Sul Ross a couple of years earlier and was a world-class sprinter. I really didn't know George because he was new, and we had eighty-six players who had showed up for two-a-days.

It wasn't a common thing, but there were times when some of the players missed curfew. When freshmen missed, I usually told them they needed to wash an upperclassman's car the next day after practice. That was part of the "pecking order" or hazing treatment that all freshmen went through. It was pretty much accepted by everyone that if they were late for curfew, that was just one of the consequences.

George and his roommate were late one night, and I noticed them sitting on the steps. They knew they were late, yet they showed no concern for the rules or the fact that they were busted.

Now, no man alive made more mistakes than I did as a freshman in college. Had George or his roommate acted like they cared that they were late, or even tried to give me an excuse, it would have made a world of difference to me. But they didn't.

George was defiant. He told me he could come and go when he pleased and no one was going to tell him differently. Then he said he sure wasn't gonna wash nobody's blankety-blank car. As soon as he made that statement, we both knew what was coming. George jumped up off the steps and started toward me.

George was not an imposing presence. In fact, he was a small guy, but I had been raised to treat everyone the same. When he stood up to fight and came at me, he accepted the consequences, just like I did. He knew I had been put in charge of curfew. He knew I was a team captain and I had been given that honor by my teammates; it was not a coaching appointment. George was a freshman and he rebelled against my authority as a team captain and a senior, plain and simple.

Some may have tried to make the fight with George, who was black, a racial issue, but it wasn't—I would have hit him if he had been purple. The fight was short. It probably didn't last even one minute. We exchanged punches, and I caught him with a left hook in the face. I felt his nose break under the blow, and that was the end of the fight, but not the incident.

When the fight started, there were very few players in the courtyard of Fletcher Hall. I was told that someone hollered "Fight!" and within seconds half of the team was outside.

Coach "Flop" Parsons lived in the dorm with us, and he came out to restore order. George and I had been separated already, but George was still mad as he hollered and cussed me. Coach Parsons was afraid things might escalate, so he told everyone to get back in their rooms. By this time, Randy and I had started back to our room. We were told by some of the other players that George refused to go to his room, left the courtyard, and ran to the parking lot adjacent to the dorm.

Coach Parsons tried to find George to see if he needed medical attention. It was at this point that one of the players hollered that "George said he had a gun and he's going to shoot Flynt." Coach Parsons came to our room and told Randy and me what was being said, and he wanted us to lock the door and stay in our room. Whether or not George actually said that, I don't know.

Randy said he saw the concern in Coach Parson's eyes. I remember Randy screaming at Coach Parsons, "Oh yeah, I'm just gonna go to bed and go to sleep while some guy is running around out there with a gun, threatening to shoot my roommate!"

Coach Parsons locked down the dormitory and everyone started to return to their rooms. I overheard Coach Parsons tell some of the players who remained in the courtyard to get back to their rooms, and that he'd called the police and the police would take care of George.

Whether the police actually came to the dorm that night, I don't know. I did not talk with, nor did I see, any police officers. I was confined to my room for the rest of the night.

Early the next morning Coach Parsons knocked on my door and told me I needed to go down to the field house and see Coach Harvey in the coaches' locker room.

Randy and I jumped into his car and pulled up in front of the coaches' locker room. When Randy and I arrived, I noticed that the entire team was huddled in the back corner of the practice field. I just glanced at them, but I thought that was weird. I knew this was about the fight with George the night before. I also knew that I had been in worse trouble than this many times. I figured the coaches were probably going to give me a stern warning and run me half to death or something.

Coach Parsons had pulled in behind us as we got out of Randy's car. He told Randy to stay outside, but he told me to go inside the locker room. I walked in, and Coach Harvey and the assistant coaches were there. Coach Harvey pointed to a chair in the middle of the room and told me to have a seat.

I sat down and faced Coach Harvey. He spoke in a matter-of-fact tone.

"Mike, we are going to have to ask you not to be part of our team this year."

I sat there dumbfounded. I couldn't speak; I couldn't believe what I had just heard. But the reality of what he had just said—the finality of it—settled in and started to overwhelm me. I just dropped my head and started to cry. I hadn't cried like that since I was a little boy and Grandpa Flynt died. I was so overcome I couldn't speak. I was embarrassed because of it, and that only made it worse.

Coach Harvey finally asked me how many hours I needed to graduate. I still couldn't speak, so I held up two fingers.

Coach Harvey asked, "Twenty?"

I shook my head and raised my two fingers again, and he clarified, "Two? You only need two hours to graduate?" I nodded, and he said, "Well, we've been told you can go to any accredited college or university in the nation to take your last hours, and you will still get your degree from Sul Ross, but you can't come back to school here."

I finally regained my composure, and I asked Coach Harvey as I pointed to the field, "Coach, have you talked to those guys out there about this? Have you asked them what they think?"

He said, "I don't need to ask them what they think. I know what they think, Mike, but I have no choice in this matter. I haven't talked to them, and you are not going to talk to them either."

I said, "Coach, that's my team. They'll do anything I ask them to do. They'll do it for me."

He looked down at the floor, shook his head, and told me that Dr. McNeil, the president of the college, had been called by the police the night before about the fight at the dormitory.

Coach Harvey said, "Mike, he called me early this morning and told me he had heard your name for the last time. He basically told me, 'It's either you or Mike Flynt. What's it going to be?' So I don't have any choice."

I became desperate.

I looked at him and said, "Coach, you know that is my team. I take care of them. I don't let them mess with anyone, and I don't let anyone mess with them."

I tried to keep my teammates away from problems and potential trouble. When I made that decision, I ended up in trouble myself sometimes. But I didn't want to see my teammates get into an altercation where they might get hurt. Everyone who knew me knew that I was a good person and would do anything I could for people. I did not start fights, and I hadn't started this one. Almost every altercation I had at Sul Ross was because someone needed me to come to their aid, and I did—no questions asked. That's just who I was.

Coach Harvey apologized but told me that I needed to call my dad and have him meet me somewhere on the highway between Alpine and Odessa. The assistant coaches would drive me partway to Odessa.

I telephoned my dad at his cabinet shop, and one of his employees put him on the phone. I said, "Dad, you need to come to Monahans and meet me. The coaches are going to take me that far, but I need a ride the rest of the way home."

He said, "Give you a ride home? What are you talking about?"

I said, "I've been kicked out of school and off the football team."

"Kicked out! For what?!"

"For fighting."

Dad said, "For fighting?" Then he started in on me, and I interrupted him.

I said, "Hey, I am exactly what you made me."

There was a pause, and Dad answered, "Okay, I'll send Bill to pick you up."

Dad never said anything else to me about the incident, ever.

I made one last appeal to Coach Harvey. I asked him to not do this to me; it was my senior year. He said, "Mike, I don't have a choice."

The coaches escorted me out of the locker room, and we bumped into

Randy. He had been told to stay outside with the other players, but he refused. As soon as he saw me, he started screaming and cussing at the coaches. He knew I was gone. Coach Krhut was trying to calm Randy down as I got in the car with the graduate assistant coaches and left.

Years later Randy told me about a trip that he and Coach Harvey made to Midland for a banquet. Randy mentioned my fight with George to Coach Harvey, and Coach told Randy what he told me that morning in the locker room: "Dr. McNeil gave me no choice; it was me or Mike Flynt." He also told Randy that kicking me off the team was the most difficult thing he ever had to do in coaching.

I left Sul Ross that day and wasn't given an opportunity to tell my team-mates good-bye. I wouldn't see some of them for thirty-six years; some I'd never see again.

Three weeks later, George quit the Sul Ross football team. I was told he said he hated that I had been kicked off the team because of that incident.

SEVEN COACH FLYNT

I sat in silence as the highway stretched out in front of me across the empty West Texas landscape. My mind raced as I tried to sort out what had just occurred over the past few hours.

I didn't dread facing my parents back home. I figured they'd understand, and besides, nothing could be worse than what I had just gone through. But I decided on that ride to Odessa that I wouldn't stay there long. There was nothing at home for me but constant reminders of what I had just lost.

I knew I would have to explain myself a thousand times, why I was home and why I wasn't playing football. Reliving the experience again and again was not something I wanted to do. I needed to move where no one knew me. Where there would be no questions asked.

After about two weeks in Odessa, I talked to my good friend Mike Campbell. He had just graduated from Pan American College and decided to move to Austin. Austin sounded like the perfect place for me to start over, so I loaded up with Mike and left Odessa. I would never live there permanently again.

Mike and I rented a room in a boardinghouse on campus at the University of Texas. I worked construction jobs during the day and washed dishes at a sorority house a few nights a week—I got to eat free that way. Those initial months away from Sul Ross, football, and my teammates were a constant reminder of a very difficult experience that wouldn't go away. I couldn't shake the memories. I was frustrated and lost.

Things also happened to me that I am sure other people would let slide. I just wouldn't do that.

I was walking back to the boardinghouse one night after washing dishes at the sorority house. There had been a basketball game at UT and the crowd had just let out. As I walked between two parked cars, this guy in a sports car on my left honked his horn. I jumped several feet straight up and out into the road.

I really thought it was funny because I had scared people like that before and could only imagine how silly I must have looked when he honked that horn.

This guy lowered his window and said, "Hey, that's a good way to get your legs broken."

I couldn't believe it. He had honked his horn at me as I walked between two parked cars, and now he told me he might have broken my legs and I needed to be more careful. I stopped, looked at him, and said, "That's a good way for you to get your butt kicked."

He just stared at me and revved the engine on his car. I turned to walk away, but the mind games had started. I knew what he was going to do, and that is exactly what he did. He backed his car up so he had a straight shot out of the parking space. He started cussing at me as he began to pull out.

I was ready. Just as he gassed his car, I spun around and kicked the rear wheel well all the way into the tire of the car. Sparks flew, and he hit the brakes. I let him get out of his car and on his feet but didn't say anything to him. He looked at his fender and then came at me.

It was over in a hurry. I looked at the other guys in the car and asked if they had anything they wanted to say to me. They shook their heads no. I left their friend on the hood of his car and walked the rest of the way to my room.

I remember thinking that night, *I wish he hadn't done that; I wish he hadn't put me in that position. Why do things like this always happen to me?* I thought it was strange, but I had never felt that way before. I wanted to change, to stop the mind games and have a calmer spirit. That motivation came in the form of a beautiful young coed from the University of Texas.

It was a mixed blessing when I first arrived in Austin. No one knew who I was, but then I didn't know anyone either. Then I remembered Eileen.

I'd first met her through Randy, who knew her from Midland, where they had both lived. Eileen and I had spent only a few hours together in the late summer of 1971, before I had to leave for two-a-days at Sul Ross, but I thought she was the most beautiful girl I had ever met. She'd actually just won a beauty contest right before we met, and I couldn't quit thinking about her.

Then it hit me—Eileen goes to UT.

I finally found a number for her, gave her a call, and took her out. She was more attractive than I remembered—she was witty, athletic, and so enjoyable to be with. Eileen was truly a gorgeous woman, but it was the optimistic, carefree young girl in her that forever captured my heart. We quickly became a regular item.

Eileen was nineteen and I was twenty-three when we started to date. She had lived on both sides of the state rivalry between Texas and Oklahoma. She was born in Abilene, Texas, but moved to Oklahoma City for high school when her father's job with Exxon took the family there. Her father was transferred to Midland after Eileen graduated from high school. She had decided to enroll at the University of Texas in Austin.

We spent more and more time together during the fall of 1971, and by the early spring of 1972 we were dating seriously. I was truly smitten. It's hard to describe the thrill it would give me—and still does—every time she smiled at me.

For her twentieth birthday in February, we headed to New Orleans with some friends to experience Mardi Gras. It was there that I raised the question of marriage, though in a rather unromantic way. I just turned to her and asked, "We are going to get married, right?" I gave her a pearl necklace for her birthday, right there on Bourbon Street, at precisely midnight. A bunch of drunks joined me in singing "Happy Birthday" to her.

I'd like to think I was a little more debonair than that, but I have a feeling her recollection is probably right-on. Thankfully, she was thinking along those same lines, and she agreed to be my wife.

I felt incredibly lucky. Had I been a religious man at the time, I would have considered myself blessed beyond my wildest dreams. Not only was Eileen an amazing woman, but her family welcomed me from day one. Some men want nothing to do with their in-laws. I was just the opposite. I absolutely adored Eileen's family. Her mother, Marie, was just a saint and always glad to see me. Her sister, Becky, was really sweet to me as well.

Eileen's father, R. A. Brand, was an amazing man. He had been in World War II and, like my dad, had been part of the D-Day invasion force, the Battle of the Bulge, and other major campaigns. He went in on day two at Utah Beach and was later awarded a Bronze Star for his bravery. But he and my dad were two totally different men. Where Dad was a rough-and-tumble kind of guy, Eileen's father was soft-spoken and serious. He was one of the wisest men I had ever met, as well as a loving husband and father. We got along extremely well.

It was through Eileen and my involvement in her world that my thoughts about violence started to fade. We married in the fall of 1972, just a little over a year after I'd been kicked out of Sul Ross. I was determined to clean up my act and settle down, because that is what she expected of me. Even though I outweighed her by almost one hundred pounds, I always said that Eileen was the only person I was ever afraid to mess with.

We lived nearly a year in Arlington, Texas, between Fort Worth and Dallas. I got a job selling insurance in Lubbock, so we headed west. Our first daughter, Delanie, was born in Lubbock in May 1974. Delanie was still a baby when we decided to make another move.

Eileen was an English major in college and had been a straight-A student. She wanted a career that would allow her to use those skills but would also compensate her fairly for the hours she put in. While she was pregnant with Delanie she researched the specialized skill of court reporting. As soon as Delanie and Eileen were both up to moving, we headed back to Arlington so Eileen could enroll in Dallas Court Reporting College.

We had a great arrangement. I watched Delanie while she was in class, and Eileen watched her in the evenings while I made cabinets. There was a large cabinet manufacturing plant outside of Arlington that provided shift work. The hours were perfect for our arrangement, and the pay was good.

I was grateful for the cabinet-making skills I had learned from my dad, but I also knew this was not something I wanted to do on a permanent basis. Eileen and Delanie were the new focus in my life, and I loved being a husband and a dad.

But I was still haunted by the mind games.

My interest in physical fitness didn't end with my football career at Sul Ross. I looked at training as a commitment and not a chore. I continued to lift weights because I enjoyed it and I couldn't stand the thought of letting myself go after all the years of working and training to please my dad.

There's a saying that "good things happen to those who are prepared." I finally had a stroke of good luck in 1976 as I lifted weights in a local gym. I noticed a guy in a University of Arkansas sweatshirt. He looked about my age, twenty-eight or so, and I wondered if we'd been at Arkansas at the same time in 1967. I asked him about it.

He answered no, but added that his former assistant was a coach at Arkansas and he had sent him the sweatshirt. I asked, "What kind of coach?"

He said, "Strength coach."

I asked him where he coached, and he answered, "The University of Nebraska." His name was Boyd Epley.

Boyd had been a track star at Nebraska in the 1960s. He and I immediately struck up a conversation about weight-training exercises and techniques. I was really intrigued, and it was like a light flicked on in my head. I told myself at that moment, *That's what I want to be, a strength coach*. It was the perfect fit for me, and I think Boyd realized it too. Three days later he offered me a job to join him as a graduate assistant strength coach at the University of Nebraska.

At the time, strength coaching was a new concept. Epley had started to develop a strength and conditioning program for the Huskers' football team.

When we met, Epley was actually in Arlington for the National Weight Lifting Competition; one of his athletes from Nebraska was entered in the competition. I was like most weight-training enthusiasts: I learned how to lift in the gym from guys who had picked up bits and pieces from different locations. There was no real science behind my training at that time.

I told Eileen about this great opportunity and my conversation with Boyd. She was all excited and said, "What are you going to do?" I told her I was going to coach. I just needed to finish my two hours at UT-Arlington and we could go to Nebraska. Eileen said, "Wait a minute . . . go where?"

I said, "To Nebraska, the University of Nebraska."

Boyd didn't need me in Lincoln, Nebraska, until that December. It worked out great, because I needed that extra time to earn my bachelor of science degree—Sul Ross officials actually cleared it so I could receive my diploma from Sul Ross.

Eileen graduated in December and passed the state certification test. There were a few states where the test was so comprehensive that if you passed it you were automatically awarded national certification by the National Court Reporters Association, and Texas happened to be one of those states. It worked out perfectly. I had my degree and Eileen was able to work as a court reporter in Nebraska. We packed our U-Haul and headed to Lincoln, where we found a small home to rent.

Nebraska football was on a roll in the mid-1970s. The Cornhuskers entered the 1976 season ranked No. 1 in the Associated Press preseason poll, but they opened the regular season with a 6-6 tie against Louisiana State. That was really viewed as a defeat because it caused Nebraska to tumble from the top spot and try to play catch-up the remainder of the year.

Nebraska also was known to have one of the largest walk-on programs for football in the nation at that time. The program had as many as two hundred walk-ons each season, which was in large part because of Boyd's strength-training program. Many of the players had scholarship offers at other schools, but they wanted to play for Nebraska. They knew they would get a fair opportunity because Boyd's training helped them prepare physically.

Boyd's system was very structured. He applied a concept called circuit training, where players moved from one exercise to another and worked different muscle groups. I had never seen circuit training or heard of that concept before I arrived at Nebraska. Boyd also informed me that our program was better described as "strength training" than weight training because of the various things we did with weights to enhance strength and maximize athletic ability.

Boyd had different types of circuits where players concentrated on heavy, explosive lifts. There was also a circuit that applied lighter lifts and conditioning. The sessions were twenty to thirty minutes max, and the players were finished. Boyd planned each exercise down to the very last second. He was extremely efficient. He made cassette tapes for the players to listen to. These tapes told them when to exercise, when to rest, when to move to the next station.

I was thrilled about the opportunity and eager to learn as much as possible about Boyd's concept of strength training. Boyd's approach to teaching was also a perfect fit for me. He carefully explained how he wanted things done and then allowed me to jump in and sink or swim.

I thought I might drown my first day on the job at Nebraska.

I was excited about my first day as a Nebraska coach when I arrived at the coliseum. I really looked the part too. Boyd had given me my coaching clothes, and I was decked out in the Cornhusker colors of scarlet and cream from head to toe.

As football players headed off the practice field, they entered a tunnel that took them either to the locker room or to the weight room. Boyd stationed me at the end of that tunnel to direct players into the weight room. Boyd said, "You stand right here at this intersection. When they come off the field, some of them may try to go straight to the locker room. When they do, you cut them off and tell them they've got to get their weight workout in first. These guys know they're supposed to work out, so you shouldn't have any problems getting them to the weight room. When you get everyone in there, make sure they follow the program."

I said, "Okay."

Like anyone put in a position of authority over people who don't know you—particularly men with high levels of testosterone—things were a little uncomfortable for them as well as for me. I stood there exactly as Boyd instructed and directed the players into the weight room. "Come on, you've got to go work out." The guys turned and headed to the weight room; they knew what they were supposed to do.

But one guy headed toward the locker room and totally ignored me. I called to him a second time and again mentioned that he needed to work out before hitting the showers. Finally, before he got out of reach, I caught the back of his jersey and said, "Hey, you need to—" That was all I got out of my mouth. He jerked around in a "swim" move, throwing his arm up and over, and knocked my hand off his jersey. He cussed me and told me to keep my hands off him. And he started toward me.

I reacted. He had taken his helmet off, and I grabbed him around the head. He was a big kid, a junior All-American center named Tom Davis. One of the assistant offensive line coaches and a few of the players separated us. The coach looked at me and said, "Who in the hell are you?" I told him I was Boyd's new assistant. He just stared at me for a few seconds and said, "Do you know where Coach Osborne's office is?"

I said, "No, sir."

He said, "You go down to the end of the hall, up those stairs, and his office is at the top. You need to go see Coach Osborne right now."

I thought, *Okay, I am at Nebraska for one day and I am going to lose my job.* My mind raced as I walked those stairs to see Coach Osborne, the highly respected and very successful head football coach at the University of Nebraska. Coach Osborne hung up his telephone as I walked into his office. His face was as red as a Coca-Cola can, and I could tell he was hot. He asked, "Who are you?"

I said, "I'm Mike Flynt; I'm Boyd Epley's new assistant."

He said, "I need you to explain yourself to me."

I said, "Well, Coach Osborne, I realize that I made a mistake." He just stared at me. I continued, "When I quit my job in Texas, moved my wife and daughter up here to Nebraska, I was excited about the opportunity to coach at Nebraska. I realize now that I really messed up. I've been in athletics most of my life, and I cannot imagine ever talking to one of my coaches the way this young man downstairs just talked to me. If it means that I have to put up with that kind of abuse to take advantage of the Nebraska experience, then I've just made a big mistake. I never should have moved my family here."

The color just drained from Coach Osborne's face. "What exactly did he say to you?" he asked. I told him everything that Tom had said. Coach answered, "Mike, you didn't make a mistake. I am sorry that this happened to you. You go back downstairs and do your job. I guarantee you something like that will never happen again." I went back downstairs to the weight room and supervised the weight-training session.

The next day, Tom Davis approached me in the weight room and shook hands with me. He said, "Your name is Mike, right?"

I said, "Yes, it's Mike Flynt."

He said, "I am really sorry about what happened yesterday, and it will never happen again." From that day until I left Nebraska, Tom and I got along great and he was a real pleasure to coach.

For years after I left Nebraska people asked me about Coach Osborne. I always told them he is one of those rare people that you see interviewed on television and think to yourself, *I wonder if he's really that nice of a guy?* Well, he is. He is one of the most genuinely nice people I have ever met, as well as one of the most impressive.

As I worked on my master's degree in physiology of exercise, I taught beginning and advanced weight-lifting classes at Nebraska. It was a tremendous experience that only reinforced the decision I had made to become a strength coach. I knew this is what I needed to do professionally. It was what I was good at, and I could help people learn how to help themselves. It was such a great feeling to get up each day and go do something I was so passionate about. And not only was it my job, but I also got to work out every day. What a bonus.

I made very little money as a graduate assistant, so Eileen was our primary breadwinner. Based on recommendations from the Court Reporting College and her résumé, she had been hired to supervise a court reporting firm in Lincoln called McIntyre and Associates. Thanks to Eileen's hard work and impressive salary, I was able to take full advantage of the Nebraska experience.

————————

The University of Nebraska had a successful athletic program for men and women. I had never trained women before, and it was rewarding. Not only were they hard workers, but they were grateful for the opportunity to train. Unlike the men, the women didn't have a lot of bad lifting habits to break, because most of them had never lifted in high school. Their bodies responded quickly to the regular strength-training routine, and their confidence and performance improved with their strength. Once again this was an area that Boyd Epley pioneered, and the Nebraska strength-training program started to gain national attention.

Other major universities across the nation began to implement strength training into their athletic programs, and I started to attract interest too. I had barely completed my first year at Nebraska when offers from other universities arrived. I interviewed at Michigan State and at the University of Oregon.

Oregon made me a very good offer, and I liked Rich Brooks, the head football coach. I talked with Boyd, and he thought it was a good career move for me, so I took all the facts to Eileen. The assistant athletic director at Oregon had assured me that with Eileen's impressive credentials, she would have no problem finding a job in Eugene. We accepted their offer, and the University of Oregon made me the first strength and conditioning coach in the Pac-10 Conference.

In January 1978, the university sent a moving company to our house to pack all of our belongings. Eileen and I loaded up Delanie, who was now three years old, and headed for Eugene, located in the southern end of Oregon's famous Willamette Valley. For a kid from the dry, mesquite-covered oil fields of West Texas, I thought we had moved to the garden of Eden. Everything was so green. With Oregon's snowcapped mountains, magnificent waterfalls, lakes, and rivers, as well as the Pacific Coast, Eileen thought it was the most beautiful place she had ever seen. She said it was like driving in a postcard everywhere you went.

Strength training had become an important component to team preparation at the Division 1 level. I took what I learned from Boyd and implemented his circuit training at Oregon. I also made my own cassette tapes for players that included the theme song "Gonna Fly Now" from the *Rocky* movie.

I was responsible for the strength-training programs for all fourteen men's and women's intercollegiate sports programs. Although Oregon was competitive in all sports, cross-country and track and field enjoyed the most success at that time.

Those programs produced running sensation Steve Prefontaine, who trained under Coach Bill Bowerman and won three consecutive Division I NCAA cross-country championships and four straight three-mile titles in track and field from 1970 through 1973. This helped spark the running boom all over the nation. Prefontaine died at the age of twenty-four in a car accident near the Oregon campus in 1975. A very popular and extensive jogging trail in Eugene is named after him, "Pre's Trail."

I worked for a year at Oregon under Rich Brooks, who had accepted his first head coaching position at the University of Oregon in 1977. Rich was a great coach, and I had a good situation at the school and complete cooperation from all the coaches. Eileen got a court reporting job with an old and prestigious family-owned firm, Tremaine and Associates, in Eugene. We loved the beautiful Northwest.

In late 1978 Oregon officials alerted me that they had given new Texas A&M football coach, Tom Wilson, permission to talk with me. I asked, "What about?" They said, "Well, he's going to offer you a job at Texas A&M. The same job you have here, as head strength and conditioning coach for all sports." I said, "I don't want that telephone call. I am not interested in that job." They said, "Well, we've already given him permission. Now that's great if you want to tell him you don't want to go, but that's your decision. Just make sure to talk to us after you've talked to Tom."

One of our assistant football coaches asked me if I was interested in the Texas A&M job, and if I would be going to interview if asked. I said, "No, I am not. I've worked for a year here, seven days a week, to get this program exactly where I want it, and now I am ready to really start cranking with these athletes. I've gotten all of them trained. We've worked out the kinks in technique with all the sports—swimmers, wrestlers, all across the board. I don't want to start over somewhere else."

The coach asked, "Mike, how many interviews have you been on? How many have you had?"

"Well, I went up to Michigan State and then I came to Oregon, so two. I loved it here, so I came to Oregon."

He said, "Make the trip for the experience, Mike. You need to do that. You need the experience." I thought that was probably wise advice.

Soon after Coach Wilson telephoned me and said, "We've heard great things about you from Boyd Epley at Nebraska. We'd like to fly you down here and show you our facility."

Coach Brooks called me into his office and asked, "So, you're going to interview?"

I said, "Yes, I am going to take a look."

He said, "Promise me one thing. Before you make a commitment, you'll come back to me first."

I said, "I promise, Coach. I'm not looking to go anywhere else; I'm not looking for another job."

But when I flew into College Station, Texas, and saw the university, I was blown away. I had heard about the Aggies and their money and tradition, and it was true. As I toured the campus with Coach Wilson and other officials, they said, "We are going to build a brand-new athletic facility; we've already got the money. Here are the plans for it." They showed me the existing facility, which was adequate but needed work.

I said, "I will need several thousand dollars' worth of equipment right away. I can't even start with what you've got here."

They said, "Just tell us what you need. We will have it here when you get here."

I asked about a courtesy car. They said, "You get a new car every four months. We trade it back to the dealership because they don't want to get too many miles on it before they sell it."

I said, "A new car every four months?" They answered yes and told me I would get to eat at the football training table every day as well.

I sat there nearly dumbfounded. I clicked off the things in my head that I had tried to get accomplished at Oregon. Oregon officials had promised me a new vehicle when they hired me, but I never got one. They kept "trying to work it into the budget." Also, I did not have access to the football training table. Texas A&M didn't know my salary at Oregon, but they said, "We want to make you an attractive offer, so we figured we would double your salary. We'll also give you an American Express card to use whenever you travel so all your expenses will be paid by the university."

They asked me if I would have to sell my house in Oregon; I told them that we rented. They said by the time I arrived in College Station they would have someone available to take Eileen and me to look at houses. They could introduce us to a banker in town to assist us in obtaining financing so we could go ahead and move in shortly after arriving from Oregon. We would be buying a home—no more renting!

As soon as I got to the airport to return to Oregon, I called Eileen and said, "Get packed."

She said, "What?"

Eileen had been upset at the thought of moving to Oregon because it took her so far away from her family, now back in Oklahoma. And now she had fallen in love with the Northwest. But I was so overwhelmed by Texas A&M's offer that I had already made up my mind this is what I wanted to do. Eileen agreed. I went back to Coach Brooks and the Oregon officials and said, "I have to take this job. I am a fool if I don't take it."

Coach Brooks asked, "What did they offer?" I told him everything and he said, "Okay, we'll match their offer." I couldn't believe what I just heard.

I said, "Coach, I've been waiting for months to get the car I was promised. I've been working seven days a week, ten to twelve hours a day with all the sports, not just football. If you matched their offer, I would feel like there is something more I need to do to earn that. I can't do any more. I can't give any more than I've been giving. Why didn't you make me an offer like this before I left? I'm sorry, Coach, but I'm going to Texas A&M. I know you would have to do the same thing in my position."

It was January 1979 when we arrived in Bryan/College Station. One of A&M's alumni, Joe Courtney, was a local home builder in College Station. We talked, and I told him we wanted to purchase a home but we needed something to rent until we could save enough for a down payment. He said, "Well, let me take you out and show you some places." He showed Eileen and me some homes he had built and said, "Here's one that is ready to move into right now. We just finished this one. If you want it, it's yours." I said, "I will have to see about trying to get a down payment." He said, "Don't worry about that; I'll get you the money for that. If you want to move in here, you let me know, and we'll get the final prep on this and you have your moving van bring your stuff here."

Eileen was really excited. Things at A&M could not have gone better for the first few months. We were close to school being out for the summer, and I had been really busy putting together training manuals for the football players to take home for the summer. Delanie was starting kindergarten in the fall, and Eileen had already begun doing freelance work at the local courthouse and for attorneys in Bryan/College Station. And while I was at Texas A&M, our son Micah was born.

The Aggies' weight room was open daily until 10:00 p.m. for both students and athletes. Each night I picked up thousands of pounds in cast-iron plates and chained them together because the students stole the plates as fast as I bought them. I ran a chain through the plates at the end of each day and locked them up. It took a lot of time and energy to collect and stack tons of plates each night. I finally decided that something had to change.

I went to our athletic director, Marvin Tate, and said, "Somebody's stealing our plates. The players aren't stealing them, because they can use them anytime they want to. I think the students are stealing them, because they can come in only during the afternoons and evenings. I have to leave for short periods between 6:00 and 10:00 p.m., and that's when the weights are disappearing. I am losing five- and ten-pound plates every day."

He said, "Well, what do you want to do about it?"

I said, "With your permission I would like to start closing the weight room at 6:00 p.m. instead of keeping it open until 10:00."

Tate said, "If you want to close it at 6:00, go ahead. That's your area. You're the head coach down there. You make that decision."

I posted signs and closed the weight room at six o'clock each night. Finals had started too, and there weren't that many students or athletes coming in to work out. Several days later it was about ten minutes before six when I started to pick up plates and clean the weight room to close up for the night.

A few freshman football players had just finished their workouts. I was ready to lock up when this big guy—I heard later he was six foot five and 285 pounds—walked in. I had never seen him before. I walked over to him and said, "I am locking up in about ten minutes." He didn't acknowledge me at all. It was like he didn't hear a word I said. He walked down the steps and put a bar on the rack and started to load it with weights.

I thought, *What's going on with this guy?*

I wasn't really in a rush, so I took my time as I cleaned. As other people walked in, I said, "We're closing up; we're locking up." So now there was nobody in the weight room except myself, a new assistant of mine named Mike Foreman, a few athletes, and this big guy. It was about ten or fifteen minutes after six, and I was ready to lock the door. The big guy walked up the steps and out the door, and I thought, *Well, I guess he's just going to leave the bar loaded up. Okay, that's cool. I will tear it down and put the bar and plates up myself.*

When I walked up to lock the door, the guy had turned around outside and was headed back into the weight room. This was the second or third time that I had told him, "Hey man, look, I'm locking up." I was in midsentence when he walked up to me on the stairs, started poking his finger in my chest, and said, "I heard what you said."

I had seen men do that to other guys in anger before, and it always ended in a fight.

This time was no different.

I hit him, and he rolled down the stairs. I followed him down the stairs into the weight room. When he started to get up, I thought, *I can't let this guy get up*. I kicked him and I hit him again, but he still got up. He grabbed a weight-lifting belt and swung it at me. I ducked, and Kenny Davidson, a freshman football player from Abilene Christian College who was in the weight room at the time, ran by from behind him and jerked the belt from his hand. I stepped in, and we exchanged punches. I finally got the best of him, and he went down again. He had caught me with a right cross on the side of the face. I knew as hard as he hit me I could not let him get up again. I remember I could barely talk for a few days after that because my jaw was so sore.

We kept at it, but he finally said, "I've had enough—I've had enough. I quit." I stepped back so he could get on his feet, and he walked out the door. His head was bleeding pretty badly where I hit him the first time. I was completely exhausted, and my jaw was killing me—he had been a major challenge.

As he walked out and headed around the building, an older guy walking by asked me, "What the heck happened to Frank?"

I said, "Who?"

He said, "That's Frank. What happened to him?"

I later found out Frank was a former All-American at Texas A&M who was now in the NFL. The remaining football players left and, of course, they headed straight for their dormitory; word about the fight started to spread. The players were saying, "When Coach Flynt tells you to do something, you'd better do it or he'll kick your butt!"

I went home, and as I was telling Eileen about the fight, the head football trainer, Billy Pickard, called me. He said, "Listen, you have to tell me that something is not true. Did you whip Frank? That didn't happen, right?"

I answered, "Well, I don't know who it was that I fought, but, yeah, I did get the best of a big guy in the weight room."

He said, "For four years I've picked pieces of beer bottle out of that guy's head. He's whipped everybody in College Station."

I said, "Billy, I don't know what to tell you; I don't know who he was. I've never seen the guy before."

He asked, "Does Coach Wilson or Marvin Tate know about this?" I said, "No, I am getting ready to call them." Billy told me they were together at a conference in Montana and gave me a telephone number where I could reach them.

I thought, *Well, here I go again. I am going to get fired because this guy was an All-American here. The alumni are going to be up in arms about this.*

I telephoned Coach Wilson about the fight, and he asked, "Are you sure it was Frank?"

"That's what everybody keeps saying, Coach. I don't know who it was, but here's what happened."

Coach Wilson said, "Mike, don't worry about it. You don't worry about anything. We'll be home in a couple of days."

Everything blew over, and I never saw Frank again. I always felt it was unfortunate that I didn't get to know him under different circumstances. He was an outstanding football player and a great athlete.

We might have been pretty good friends.

EIGHT A LIGHT IN THE MIDST
OF DARKNESS

When Tom Wilson hired me as the program's strength and conditioning coach, I felt Texas A&M was the perfect fit. The university had blueprints for a new athletic facility, the athletics program was committed to strength and conditioning, and I was determined and excited to help make a difference with our student athletes.

Football was serious business in the state of Texas, and it wasn't any different at A&M. We finished 6-5 and in fifth place in the Southwest Conference in Coach Wilson's first full year in 1979, which was highlighted by a 13-6 victory over sixth-ranked Texas in our regular season finale at home.

We had hoped that victory would give us needed momentum during the 1980 season, but that wasn't the case. We finished the season with a 24-14 win over archrival Texas, but a 4-7 overall record didn't sit well with school administrators, fans, and boosters. The memory of fifteen losing seasons over a sixteen-year period from the late 1950s to the early 1970s was still fresh in the minds of many in Aggieland. The rumors were flying, and things didn't look good from a job security standpoint.

It was during the off-season of January 1981 that I was approached by a friend I had known since we were fourteen years old back in Odessa. John and I had talked on the phone a few times over the years, but I hadn't seen him since 1975.

I knew from past conversations that he was in the "rag business," as he called it, which meant he was a wholesale buyer and seller for large clothing retailers. He had taken his business to the next level and now sold

American-made clothing in Europe and other foreign markets. He told me the demand for any clothing made in America was very high in foreign markets and he had developed that niche in his business and had it down to a science.

A handful of our Texas A&M track and field athletes had recently participated in a meet in Russia. When they returned, all they talked about was how much money they had made when they sold their clothes to the locals. "These people offered us money just to buy the clothes we were wearing," they said. "We went through our suitcases and sold everything we had and bought their stuff to wear home." This seemed to be confirmation of everything John had told me.

Because I'd known John for so long, I trusted him completely. So we worked out an arrangement wherein I would invest money for thirty days and he'd pay me the money back, plus a 15 percent return. Eileen thought this was too good to be true, but based on my history with John, she reluctantly agreed.

A few days later I wrote him a check for $10,000. A few weeks later I received a check from him for $11,500.

I shared my newfound investment information with several of the coaches at Texas A&M. I had since learned from John that the largest and oldest law firm in Austin had also invested over one million dollars per month in his clothing business. If the clothing business was good enough for them, it was good enough for me. I jumped in with both feet.

Following John's instructions, I accepted money on his behalf from friends, family, and acquaintances. They'd give me money, which I gave to John. He'd pay me back the principal plus a 15 percent profit. I'd give 10 percent of the profits to the individual who put up the funds, and I'd keep 5 percent for facilitating the transaction.

By the end of April I was making as much as $15,000 a month from money I put up plus the 5 percent "commission." John offered me a full-time position in his company to help him manage and expand his investments. Again, the timing seemed perfect, since I was thinking Tom Wilson might be fired at A&M. Assuming the Aggies wouldn't put up with another mediocre season, I resigned from A&M—much to Eileen's chagrin—and we moved to Austin in May 1981 so I could work full-time with John.

Turns out I was right about a coaching change at Texas A&M. The coaching staff and the athletic director were fired in December 1981.

Eileen was right about the investment opportunity with my friend John. It was too good to be true.

In July 1982 John was indicted on several federal counts. I was also indicted because of my close association with him. I felt betrayed by a friend whom I had trusted with everything, and it was the start of a nightmare that lasted for almost five years.

Prior to our Sul Ross homecoming game in 2007, a reporter asked me what I felt was the biggest difference between the Mike Flynt who played in 1969 and 1970 and the Mike Flynt of 2007. That was one of the easiest questions I had been asked in an interview because it was one I had already considered many times before.

"Jesus Christ," I said. "It was the presence of Christ in my life that changed everything about me."

The change was a long time coming, and it was, perhaps, the biggest struggle of my life. I had allowed myself to be consumed by the mind games and the fighting instinct that my dad had instilled in me and that I had further cultivated. Eileen had calmed me down incredibly, but my mind never completely rested.

I was still always scanning the room for someone who might cause trouble. It had gotten to the point where with everybody I met, as we shook hands, I imagined myself in a fistfight with that person. That was the mental game I played so that, just in case it ever came to fists, I wasn't caught by surprise. It was an exhausting, stressful way to live, but after so many years, it had become my way of life.

My whole world was thrown upside down in 1982 with the indictment.

I had never faced an opponent that I couldn't tackle with my helmet and shoulder pads or hammer with my fists. But when I was accused of something I didn't do, I was suddenly faced with an adversary that was impervious to everything that had worked for me in the past. And now the stakes were greater than they had ever been before. I'd never felt this helpless, and for the first time, maybe ever in my life, I was really scared.

I had started to drink more and more as the legal issues dragged on. One afternoon I just had too much to drink, and in a moment of despair and desperation, I remarked to Eileen that maybe the best way for me to deal with this mess would be to take my pistol, go in the closet, and end this whole thing.

Eileen knew in her heart it was probably the Jack Daniels talking, but it frightened her and she knew it was time to act. She asked Delanie to watch her younger brother, Micah, took me by the hand, and we headed out our front door for a walk.

We walked down to the golf course, which was closed for the day, and Eileen began to talk with me about spiritual things. She told me how much God loved me. She also explained her relationship with Christ and how He desired to have a relationship with me, too, if I would just let Him. We had been married for ten years, yet I had never realized the depth of Eileen's love for God. She told me He had a plan for my life and would never leave me, but I had to be willing to accept Him and surrender control of my life to Him.

Surrendering control—that was something I clearly didn't see how I could do. Yet the more she talked to me about God and His love, the more things made sense. As we walked those beautiful, emerald-green fairways, I thought about the parched brown desert of West Texas and how much my life was like that land. I longed for my life to be made new and lush like that beautiful golf course after a summer rain.

But I knew nothing about God. Even though we always went to church as a family (Eileen insisted on it), I had never really listened to the preacher or given any thought to his messages. Church was just something we did on Sunday mornings. I thought it was wonderful for our children, but to be quite honest, I really didn't think it was something I personally needed.

But after Eileen talked to me that afternoon, I suddenly had a burning desire to know more about Eileen's God. She embraced me and prayed for me on the golf course that day. We cried together, and somehow I felt things were going to be different.

The next morning I tried to read the Bible.

The only way I can describe the experience was that it was like eating dry cereal. I could get through it and, with enough chewing, could finally get it to go down. But I just didn't enjoy it. I felt like something was missing. Nothing stuck with me. I'd read a page, but by the time I reached the bottom, I couldn't tell you anything about what I had just read.

So I tried a different approach—Delanie's Bible storybooks.

I have to admit I felt a little foolish as I took the first volume down from the shelf. I mean, here I was, a grown man, resorting to kids' books with simple language and pretty pictures. But I was desperate to know the peace that Eileen had in her life. She had promised me it was there for me also if I put my pride aside and asked for it.

I read the first volume, cover to cover, and then the second, and the third. By the time I finished all sixteen volumes—Genesis through Revelation—I knew the way I looked at the world would never be the same. It started to make sense to me how this series of stories—this amazing collection of writings, from so many different people across the centuries—could be brought together for one common purpose and with one goal.

I picked up my "grown-up" Bible and started to read again, and now I had a sense that I knew what I was reading and what God was trying to tell me about how to live my life. When I came across the passage about "babes in Christ," I had to laugh—that was me, no question! Even though I turned to kids' books to figure it all out, I finally began to grasp the fact that God really was everything Eileen had said He was.

I finally had hope.

It was like a light had come on and had shown me what was truly important in life. All I needed to do was trust in God and believe in His Son, Jesus. Words didn't matter and my past didn't matter—God's grace would cover that. I was His child and He was my God; everything else would just work itself out. And it did.

It took time, but God did His part.

As the legal issues progressed in Austin, we moved to Colorado so I could work with a group of geologists and geochemists whom I had met over the past eighteen months. The price of gold had risen to over eight hundred dollars an ounce, and the thought of being involved with mining intrigued me. The company, Earthsearch, would option mining properties, evaluate them, and then sell the option to a mining company if the property was commercial. It was an exciting venture for a while, but one that required a great deal of travel and time away from my family.

So our stay in Colorado was short-lived. Also, it was just too cold for us Texans. We had gone to Tennessee to visit Mike Campbell and his family for spring break in 1985. We were there only a few days and fell in love with Franklin. In June 1985 we moved to Franklin and, for the first time in a long time, we felt like we were home. It was there that our second daughter, Lily, was born.

But I needed to be back in the business of fitness. It had been a major part of my life, one that I loved. Soon after moving to Tennessee I developed a strength and conditioning program for children. My primary focus was the homeschooling market, because they had a perceived need for physical education but no curriculum. The program was named "Train Up a Child" from Proverbs 22:6, which states, "Train up a child in the way he should go: and when he is old, he will not depart from it."

The program used body weight and muscle-against-muscle exercises and allowed children and families to train together without weights or equipment. It was a workout videotape with accompanying charts and literature that I marketed to families all over the nation for more than ten years.

Finally, in 1987, after five long years, justice was served. Thankfully, I had kept meticulous records of all the money that was transferred through my account and given to John, so I had hard evidence that I had not taken anyone's money. All the charges against me were dropped, and the judge said the indictment against me was the worst miscarriage of justice he had ever seen.

John was found guilty as charged, and the nightmare for him continued. I had forgiven him for what he had done to me, and I told him so. Really, God knew exactly what it would take to get me on my knees, and for that reason I was able to look back on that whole experience as a blessing and thank Him that it happened. With the way He'd worked everything together for my good, I could honestly say it didn't happen *to* me; it happened *for* me.

As I began my journey *with* God I began to look back on my life *without* Him. I was grateful for His protection all those years I walked in violence. I was grateful I had not seriously injured or even killed someone, or someone hadn't killed me.

There were certain fights in my life that I looked back on with a sense of pride for what I had done—coming to the rescue of my friend in Colorado and stepping in on behalf of a young lady at a dance who was being harassed by a drunk. I am glad I was there and had the ability to intervene and do something to help them. On the other hand, there were so many more situations I could have avoided, so many things that might have been different, had I stopped to think about the consequences.

I knew it wasn't the fight with the freshman that got me kicked off the Sul Ross team and out of school; it was the other confrontations that had ganged up on me. Yet I'd never looked at the big picture and thought about how my actions, no matter how justifiable they were, might adversely affect other people. Instead, it was always about me and my immediate self-gratification. It was about those two or three minutes of getting what I wanted.

Looking back now, it was so obvious to me that what had defined my life was the self-induced mind games I'd played because of the edge they gave me. I felt comfortable and in control when I knew I was always mentally ready, just a second or two away from being "on," with my fists and feet flying at the slightest sign of a physical challenge. That had become my default setting. It had become automatic. Biologists talk about the "fight or flight reflex" in animals, and that was how it had been with me—except "fight" was the only option.

For almost thirty years I'd been locked in just one way of thinking, acting, and reacting. Now I understood; that was all wrong, and that was the part of me that had to change. But even as I came to the realization that I needed to change, I knew it wasn't something I could just switch off. And it wasn't anything I could do by myself.

I would have to allow God to help me.

As time went on, I caught myself creeping back into moments of weakness, when fighting was just the easier option over reason and forgiveness. That's when I realized that if I was going to truly change, and change the way I thought about things, it would be by substituting the things I learned from God's Word and having those truths on the "fingertips" of my mind every day.

Then I read a book by Chuck Swindoll called *Three Steps Forward, Two Steps Back*. It seemed to describe my situation perfectly. The mind games of violence were still there, even when I tried to suppress them. But I knew if I invested my time in Bible study and prayer, God would help me to overcome and allow me to give control to Him.

The more I did that, the more the impulse toward violence melted away. It took years, but from time to time I would suddenly realize it had been days, or weeks, since I had played a violent mind game. As I made the choice each morning to study God's Word and try and focus on His way of doing things throughout the day, I slowly but surely became a different person, and the violent thoughts that had consumed me for so many years went away.

Mike Campbell has known me as well as anyone since we were twelve years of age. Mike told me several years ago that I was the most changed person he had ever known.

I wish I could say there were no setbacks, but as with any process, there were lapses. I had become comfortable with the new me and truly felt the old Mike was forever gone. I was so wrong.

One Sunday after church, when our children were still pretty young, we stopped at a store for Micah to return a video game. Eileen had let Lily, three years old at the time, out of her car seat in the back to climb up front and sit in her lap while we waited. At the time Lily had ITP, a rare immune system disorder that caused her blood platelets to be extremely low. We were told by the doctors at Vanderbilt to not allow her to have any blows to her body as her blood wasn't clotting adequately and she could start hemorrhaging. Her platelet count at that time was only nine thousand, whereas over one hundred fifty thousand was considered normal.

After Micah got back in the car, I began to slowly ease our minivan forward to pull out, giving Eileen time to put Lily back in her car seat. Out of nowhere a guy in his late twenties steered his car straight at us. I thought he might hit us head-on, but he swerved away at the last minute. I had no choice but to hit my brakes, which threw Lily into the dashboard.

The whole family just looked at Lily and gasped, hoping she was all right. There was plenty of room for that jerk to get around us, but he laid on his horn and flipped me off as he drove by, mouthing obscenities at me with my wife and kids in the car. The thought of my little girl being hurt—not to mention his incredibly rude, blatant "in your face" actions—caused something in me to snap. I was so angry that suddenly, just like that, the old Mike was back.

I turned to Eileen and told her before she had a chance to speak, "Don't try and stop me."

I got out of the car and waved for this guy to come back. Much to my delight, he stopped and turned around. As he drove toward me, I quickly took off my tie—a past experience wearing a tie had created problems for me, and this was an automatic move. As he drove up he lowered his window and apparently thought we were going to have a verbal exchange.

Big mistake.

I walked over to his car and punched him in the face, knocking him down in the seat. He rose back up, and I knocked him down again. He then rose up just enough to see over the dashboard, hit the gas, and sped off.

I climbed back in the van and there were my children, just staring at me with their mouths open in disbelief. Suddenly, my heart dropped. I thought, *Oh, no, no. What have I done?* I immediately said, "I'm sorry." I instantly felt so bad. Delanie, seventeen years old at the time and driving herself, said, "I bet he never does that again!"

On the ride home I thought, *What if he had shot me in front of Eileen and our children? Or what if he had run over someone in the parking lot as he tried to get away from me?* I made the decision then and there that unless I was actually defending myself or my family—*actually* defending them from danger and not just from some smart aleck who wanted to show off in a parking lot—I would never resort to violence again.

That was the last time I threw a punch and, by the grace of God, I don't think I've even had the desire to throw one again.

I continue to grow each day, and there are still challenges for me from time to time—things that might not be a challenge for other people. But there is no doubt I can overcome these challenges because of who Jesus is in my life.

One of the biggest challenges in my faith early on was how to share my faith with others. I wanted to talk about my faith with my dad most of all, because I knew he struggled with many of the same issues I had struggled with for most of my life—I'd learned this behavior from him! I just knew that if I could get him to know Christ as I did, Dad would find the same forgiveness, freedom, and peace I had found.

I had never seen my dad in a church unless it was to attend a wedding or a funeral. I tried to talk with him about my newfound faith, but it just seemed to get bogged down in memories of the past. Every time I brought it up, he looked at me as if to say, "Mike, I remember all the wild things you did, the barroom fights, the times I bailed you out of jail for disorderly conduct." It was like he was saying, "I know you and I know all about you. You can't fool me with this Christianity thing."

I was reminded of Jesus when He said in the book of Mark that a prophet is without honor in his own hometown. What He was saying was that because the people in Nazareth had known Him since He was a young boy, they couldn't believe He was the Son of God. They remembered watching Him play with their children. They knew His brothers and sisters, and now He was claiming to be the Son of God? No way! I felt this was how my dad looked at me. My past spoke louder than my present, and he could only see in me the boy he had raised and knew so well. The boy who had made so many, many mistakes.

I procrastinated and continued to put off asking the tough questions about Dad's relationship with the Lord. I prayed for him daily, but I waited. Then one day I realized I had waited too long.

It was October 12, 1994, Lily's sixth birthday. It was a wet, cold, and miserable day. But I had gotten home early because I knew we wanted to do something special for Lily's birthday, and I was always excited about our children's birthdays.

As I pulled into the driveway and drove around the house to the garage, I noticed my son, Micah, was standing outside in the rain. My first thought was that he had some news about a surprise for Lily, or he was just glad to see me home a little early. Then it hit me—why would he be standing in the rain? I knew something must be wrong, so I jumped out of the truck and asked him, "Micah, is everything all right?"

"No, Dad," he said. "PaPa died today."

I dropped to my knees, and my first thought was, *Oh, God, where is he?*

It was about a fifteen-hour drive from our home in Franklin, Tennesse, to where my parents lived in Brownwood, Texas. Eileen and I loaded up the kids and headed west right away.

As I drove, I realized I couldn't cry anymore. There were no facial expressions, no sobs, just tears running down my face. I couldn't stop thinking about how many times I had almost shared the gospel with Dad but never did. It was painful to remember the story in the book of Luke about the poor man who went to heaven and the rich man who went to hell and was in great torment and pain from the flames. I knew if we did not trust Jesus while we were alive, it was too late after we died. My faith had been even further reinforced by an in-depth study of biblical prophecies that I had done; I knew that every word of the Bible was true.

When we arrived in Brownwood, we went first to the funeral home and then to the house. I was overwhelmed by my emotions, but I needed to know exactly where Dad was when he died and what he was doing. I asked Mother to show me.

She explained that he had been mowing the yard. She commented about how well he was doing with his new prosthetic leg and how he had been working out and lost twenty-five pounds. She said he wanted to surprise me. Mom said he had walked across the street to the vacant field and dumped the grass cuttings from his mower. As Mom walked by the plate-glass window in the living room on her way to put a coffee cup in the kitchen sink, she saw him. He stood facing the sunset with his hands on his hips as if he was in deep thought.

Mom put the coffee cup in the sink and walked back across the room. She looked out through the window again, and Dad was gone.

Mom told me she knew he couldn't have gotten out of her field of vision that fast, so she started across the yard to see where Dad had gone, calling his name. Then she saw his blue overalls in the low place on the other side of the road where he was lying face down. She explained that just as she reached him, a pickup truck pulled up and two men jumped out. They had seen him fall and started doing CPR right away, and kept at it until the paramedics arrived.

We walked together to the exact spot where Dad was when he fell. It was something I felt very compelled to do. As we crossed the road to that spot, a white pickup truck full of construction equipment drove past us and pulled into a driveway two doors down. As we watched two men get out of the truck, Mom grabbed my arm and said, "Mike, those are the same guys who tried to help your dad." She suggested I walk down there and thank them for what they did. I told her I would, but right now I just wanted to be alone at that spot.

Mom went back to the house, and I just stood there praying and wondering what Dad was thinking before he died. After a few minutes I walked down the street to the house where the two guys had pulled in with their truck. There was a home remodeling sign in front of the house and the door was open. I walked in, and one of the men was tying on a nail apron. He looked up and saw me. We shook hands and introduced ourselves, but he didn't release my hand.

I told him that Mother had told me what they tried to do to save Dad and that I appreciated their kindness. While he held on to my hand, the guy said, "Yes, we were there; in fact, your dad was still warm when I got to him." He told me he was a volunteer firefighter and was up-to-date on all the latest CPR techniques, and he told me my dad was dead before he hit the ground. He was gone and there was no saving him.

I thought it was a little strange that this man continued to grip my hand as we talked. But then he said, "I don't know what your relationship is with the Lord, but there is something I want to tell you."

Every muscle in my body tightened.

He said, "After that happened to your dad, I was so upset I just went home. My neighbor has his own carpet business, and he was at home that day, standing outside, so I told him what had happened. My neighbor is very outspoken for the Lord. And he asked, 'Was that Mr. Flynt up there on top of the hill at Mountain View?' And I said, 'Yeah, I think that was his name.' He said, 'You know, I was in his house two years ago replacing his carpet, and we got to talking about Jesus, so I asked him, 'Mr. Flynt, if you were to die today, do you know for certain that you'd go to heaven?'"

I could barely breathe as this man continued his story and clutched my hand. "And your dad told him, 'No, I don't.' So my neighbor said, 'You can just kneel down here with me if you want to, and we'll just take care of that right now.'"

The worker looked at me and said, "I just wanted you to know that your dad knelt that day and made a profession of faith and accepted Christ as his Savior."

The instant he told me that, I felt as if my heart had been set free. You read in the Bible where it talks about "in the twinkling of an eye." Well, when this Good Samaritan told me that about Dad, it flashed in my mind exactly where I was in every phone conversation I had had with him over the last couple of years. I recalled him saying he was praying for me at the end of each call, and I thought he was just saying that because I would tell him I was praying for him. But then I knew he was saying that because he really was praying for me. God, in His mercy, showed me my dad is in heaven and I am going to see him again.

That conversation absolutely changed my life. I didn't have to look on my father's passing with regret, because I now knew he had made his peace with God and had accepted Christ into his life. Even though I had not been able to bring myself to talk to him about that, God sent someone else to do it, and I will be forever grateful. It gave me such comfort to know he had finally surrendered his own life to Christ.

For me, that was really the moment when I felt my old self die. God had brought my life full circle. The man who had handed me those boxing gloves at age six and molded most of my life for violence had been able to make his own peace with God. And then God in His mercy had showed me that miracle in my father's life.

We are told that in Christ all things are made new.

I surely believe that.

I'm living proof.

NINE "I'M HERE TO PLAY"

I was a college senior again.

I passed my football physical with flying colors on August 9. I was five foot ten and weighed 200 pounds. My blood pressure was 128/83, and my resting pulse was 66. The doctor's assistant smiled and said, "You know those young guys will be after you." I told her I wasn't worried about it. She said, "Well, you are in great shape, so go have fun." Coach Wright was in the doctor's office too. He had his blood pressure measured at the same time they took mine. He smiled at me and asked if he could borrow my blood pressure.

I also enrolled in school. I had to take nine hours to be a full-time graduate student, and I selected what I thought were three interesting classes that would help me with my Powerbase business—Seminar in Management, Health in the Public Schools, and History of American Sport. Plus, with the help of Joy Parsons, the widow of my former assistant coach "Flop" Parsons, I found a home to rent for $1,350 a month about five miles outside of town. Coach Parsons and Mrs. Parsons had lived in the dormitory on campus with us back in the day. Now she operated a real estate agency there in Alpine. She told me she wished Coach was alive to see me play, that he would really love that. I would have loved that too, and I was especially grateful for her help.

I had a much better housing arrangement the second time around. It was a three-bedroom, ranch-style home on five acres off a gravel road in Sunny Glen Estates, which was tucked at the bottom of the Davis Mountains. I had climbed and run those same hills the last time I lived in Alpine. The view of the cacti and mountains out our front living room window was stunningly beautiful.

I met again with Coach Wright to discuss the media. He reiterated his concerns about my presence being a distraction but said he felt it was under control. He then added that if Sul Ross had been in a metropolitan area where the media had convenient access to us, he never would have been able to let me do this. Being in a remote location as we were—160 miles from the nearest airport—he figured no one would bother to come this far to find us. He was wrong about that one.

I asked him if he planned to give me an opportunity to earn a starting spot on the team. He said he would do what was best for the team. "If you are good enough to play, I'll let you play, but only I will make that decision." Then he repeated, "I'm going to do what's best for this team. If that means that Mike Flynt doesn't play, then that's what I'm going to do, but you've got a lot to prove before you can make this team."

I didn't have a problem with anything Coach said. I was back here for one reason and one reason only, and that was to help the Sul Ross football team. I hoped to do that by playing, and felt confident I would be able to. But I would help in whatever role I could. I was excited about the opportunity.

The team met at Jackson Field at one o'clock in the afternoon on August 11. The coaches passed out our equipment, and everything was pretty cool. We were in a single-file line. None of the other players said a word to me until Darren Thomas glanced over at me as he walked by. "So, you gonna coach, right?"

I said, "No, I am here to play."

He said, "To play! Man, how old are you?" I said, "I'm fifty-nine." He looked at me incredulously. "At fifty-nine?" Then he started broadcasting it to the rest of the team. "This man is fifty-nine years old and can still play." He went up and down the line and said, "Hey, come here and meet this guy."

While the players hadn't met me yet, many knew of me. One of the linebackers, Kyle Braddick, said, "Hey, we heard about you on the radio, and we just want you to know we're pulling for you."

This was my first informal introduction to my new teammates. Of course, I hoped they would see me as a teammate when I put my helmet on, and not as an "old guy" who was a grandfather and a card-carrying member of AARP. I was eight years older than our head coach, and two of my kids were older than any of my new teammates. But I just wanted to do what I had done before, and that was play football.

We started two-a-day practices on Sunday, August 12, and they were difficult. It was as hard, hot, and intense as I remembered it being thirty-seven years earlier. I worked with the linebackers and not only survived but held my own in all of the drills. I felt great about that. It was even more difficult on Monday, with more conditioning drills and contact drills. I was impressed with this team and how hard these players worked.

We stopped for a water break, and a young man came up and knelt down next to me and said, "Excuse me, sir. How old are you?"

"I am fifty-nine."

"Man, how can you be doing this? I've been watching you, and you're just doing great!"

"Well, it's by the grace of God."

"I can do all things through Christ who strengthens me," he said.

I smiled and said, "I have prayed that verse about five times today!"

He said, "Man, you've got to. This is hard." He introduced himself to me. He was Jeremy Cartwright, a freshman receiver from Killeen, Texas.

I was just another one of the guys who participated in practice and full-contact drills. I began to get to know some of the other linebackers. Nathan Graham was from Odessa Permian, so we had that immediate connection. Jarrett Ballew was from Andrews; he was soft-spoken and quiet, which was deceptive because he was a headhunter. Milo Garza and Fernie Acosta were both starters, tough and talented.

I sat with a lot of the defensive players one day at lunch and shared my story with them. I told them I hoped to make the team and help in any way I could.

Milo said, "You're already helping me."

I was impressed by all of them, their work ethic and talent. Some of the incoming freshmen linebackers were talented as well. Kyle Braddick, Derek Thompson, Brandon Hemstreet, Cole Tarleton, and Andy Mata were all very impressive.

I started to realize that it wouldn't be easy to make this team.

We ended Thursday's practice with a weight-training session that night. Then all of a sudden the coaches were hollering that they wanted to stage a lifting contest of strength and endurance. The coaches selected players to get on their backs in the middle of the weight room. Everyone was given a forty-five-pound plate. We started on the whistle and lifted the plate until we couldn't lift any more. Players with the most repetitions advanced into the next round.

The coaches selected three players for the final contest, and I was one of the three. The entire team surrounded us. We were each handed a forty-five-pound plate. As I got ready to lie back and start the contest, I looked into the crowd and saw only one face, Jeremy's. We made eye contact, and I mouthed, "Pray for me." I wasn't sure I had enough remaining strength to win this contest. And Jeremy said, "I will."

I closed my eyes and thought how this was an incredible blessing to be fifty-nine years old, back at Sul Ross, and in a situation to hopefully make an impression on my teammates. Coach blew the whistle, and we started. I knew that some of these guys had done more than two hundred reps on this exercise in the past, so I wasn't thinking about reps; I was focused on just doing it.

I had to keep going, keep lifting until I couldn't lift anymore, and hope that it was enough. After a few minutes I opened my eyes, and the guy on my right had stopped. The cheering from my teammates had intensified, and the guy on my left had started to slow down. I knew I had him beat. I continued to push. Then my teammates were yelling my name, "MIKE! MIKE! MIKE!"

The contest was over. I had won.

The place went nuts. Players lifted me up, slapped me on the back, and told me how great I had done. This was the first time I felt truly accepted by my teammates, and it was a wonderful, amazing feeling. My age was no longer an issue.

It seemed like everything from that day forward changed. The players I hadn't known in the past started to talk to me. They said hello when we saw each other on campus. I started to learn their names too. I called out their names in practice every time I saw them do something good, because I wanted them to know I knew who they were and that I was interested in how they played.

I tried to encourage as many players as I could in practice. I knew how important it was, particularly when you are young, to hear your named called, for someone to acknowledge something positive you have done. And they reminded me during that lifting contest of how great it was to hear someone call your name, at any age.

Practice was going great, but I began to experience some tightness in my groin. On one of the evening weight workouts at one station, we were stepping up on thirty-inch polymeric boxes, holding a twenty-five-pound dumbbell in each hand. We had already completed two workouts that day in pads, and in performing those step-ups, I overworked the connective tissue in my groin. I felt an immediate discomfort.

I was afraid to run full speed because I knew how devastating a groin pull can be. I talked to Coach Pendergraft about the tightness. Coach P was an associate professor and head of the equine sciences department. He was one of our volunteer coaches and worked with the defensive backs. He was also in great shape, and we had a lot of respect for him both as a coach and an athlete.

He told me he was thirty-nine years old and had pulled his groin three years ago. He said it had taken him eighteen months to get it well. "Whatever you do," he advised, "don't pull that tendon in your groin. You do and you're done for the season." I asked if he had some good horse liniment I could use. He laughed and said, "You're kidding me, right?" "Absolutely not," I replied. "If you have something that works on horses, then I'm willing to try anything to help this injury heal."

Coach P gave me some of the worst-smelling stuff you can imagine. Eileen made me sleep on the floor the whole time I was using it. The players knew precisely when I walked into the locker room. They didn't have to see me; they smelled me. But I knew the horse liniment was helping. I wasn't getting worse, and I was slowly beginning to make progress. Coach Pendergraft joked with me at practice and told me I reminded him of his horse stables.

I felt I had held my own in practice and in drills. While my groin was feeling better, I slightly injured my right shoulder in a full-contact tackling drill. The pain quickly subsided, and I didn't miss any drills or time. Coach Bridges asked me one day about the smell that followed me. I told him about the liniment and that I was doing all I could to get my groin healed so I could run full speed.

Coach said, "Hey, just between you, me, and the grass, we're pleased with what we have seen you do so far, and we're not looking to run you off."

That was a relief. The coaches weren't too free with compliments.

The following day was a long day, but Tuesday, August 21 was a great day too. Make that a *fantastic* day. That's the day Coach Wright walked up to me during practice and told me I had made the team. And then he said it again with emphasis, "I mean, you *made* this team."

I was caught off guard because it was so spontaneous and out of the blue. Coach Wright also said he planned to make an announcement to the media on Wednesday, the first day of classes. Coach said his announcement would be, "Mike is on the team, but not on the travel squad because of a slight muscle tear. I also have nine other players in the same situation."

I was disappointed that I wasn't included on the travel roster for the opener, but I understood. The main thing for me was that I had made the team! I was thrilled! I hadn't been worried about making a football team since I was in middle school.

I told Cole Tarleton, Andy Mata, Ross Guzman, and some of the other players I warmed up with before practice that I had made the team.

Pat and J.V. Flynt, Mike's parents, in their military uniforms, 1944.

The Flynt family: parents J. V. and Pat,
siblings Gwen, Mike, and Pam, 1990.

Flynt Chosen LSC
Player Of Week

Mike Flynt

Mike's senior year
at Permian High School, 1965.

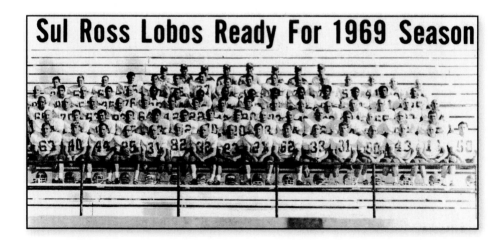

Sul Ross Lobos Ready For 1969 Season

Mike (behind tackle), Charlie Adams (died in middle of the 2007 season) and David Cooper #77 (died in June of 2008), both teammates and lifelong friends.

Mike and Randy Wilson with teammates at Fletcher Hall Athletic Dorm, 1970.

Mike with Randy Wilson at Texas A&M, 1980.

Mike with
Delanie and
Eileen, 1975.

Mike and Eileen, 1977.

Coach Larned
and Mike, 2007.

Mike with his family
after his first game,
October 13, 2007. From
left to right, Eileen,
Jennifer (daugher-in-
law), Lily, Mike,
Delanie with Collin,
and Micah.

Sul Ross "Lobo" with
Collin (grandson) and
Ben (son-in-law) at
Homecoming game.

Homecoming day
captains, 2007.

Mike in action
at Sul Ross vs.
Mississippi College,
2007.

Mike with former teammates from the 1969–1970 season.

Kneeling, left to right: Cicelio Lara, Randy Wilson, Terry Stuebing, Dewayne Richters, Stan Williamson. Standing, left to right: Don Richters, Larry Cottrell, Mike Tabola (hidden in back), Roel Maldonado, Bob Hayter (in cowboy hat) Joe Priest, Mark Hulin (in back), Mike Flynt, Gerald Trull, Erich Hardaway (hidden behind Trull), Jay Anderson, Dennis Carpenter.

Mike with Jeremy Cartwright (far right) and his family, and Jamal (J.J.) Johnson (kneeling), 2007.

Mike with some of his 2007 teammates.

(Milo Garza, Zach Gideon, Preston Watts, T.J. Barber, Coach Steve Wright, Adam Cuellar, Austin Davidson, Michael Van Wagner, Chris Vela, Chase Bowser, Andrew Ross [in back], Fernie Acosta)

Mike clowning around on his 60th birthday, 2008.

Word spread among my teammates, who immediately congratulated me and hugged me. Privately, I felt a lot of emotion. I had made the team! I couldn't wait to tell Eileen and our kids. It was really going to be a switch. After all the years of supporting each of them in different sports, I was the one now calling them to tell them I had made the team.

They were going to love it!

Coach Wright also needed to talk to me about the media. Several groups wanted to do a documentary. He asked if I wanted to consider having a documentary filmed of me during the season, where cameras followed my every move on and off the field. I told him I felt it would be disruptive to me and our team. He completely agreed and was glad we were on the same page.

Coach also reminded me about the first time I met him in July, when I had asked him if I could try out for his team. After I'd finished running with the freshmen, he'd told me he needed to sleep on it and he would give me an answer the next day. He said that what he should have told me was that he needed to pray about it. He admitted he had become very spiritual since his oldest daughter had developed some health problems. But Coach said I had answered the three questions in his mind that allowed him to give me a chance. He also said he trusted me and decided that we'd speak to the media together later that day.

It's truly difficult to describe my feelings after I was told I had made the team. The realization that my dream had at last come true was still hard to believe. It had been so many years.

It was living by Dad's three rules that had gotten me kicked out of Sul Ross in 1971. It was answering Coach's three questions that allowed me a second chance at Sul Ross in 2007.

I needed to telephone Coach Larned and tell him the good news.

TEN PATIENCE IS A VIRTUE

Things for me were not going as planned for our season opener at Texas Lutheran University.

As my teammates prepared to take the field against TLU on September 1, 2007, Eileen and I were guests at the campus home of Sul Ross State University president Dr. Vic Morgan. Dr. Morgan and his wife, Mary Jane, invited us for dinner and to listen to our six o'clock game on the radio.

I was frustrated and disappointed that I wasn't healthy enough to dress out and be with my team in Seguin, Texas, but I knew I had to be patient. Too many times I had seen players succumb to pressure and try to come back and play before they were ready, and the result was almost always the worst-case scenario.

We had an enjoyable visit with Dr. Morgan, and Eileen made a new friend in Mary Jane. I jokingly told them that the last time I was called by the president of Sul Ross, it had not been for an invitation to dinner but rather for an invitation to leave town. Dr. Morgan has a great sense of humor, and we had a wonderful time as we visited and listened to the game.

Dr. Morgan was appointed the university's tenth president in 1990 and was the first president of Sul Ross to come from within the ranks of the university. (His tenure at Sul Ross had begun in 1975 when he joined the university in the mathematics department.) Despite my reputation and troubles with the previous school administration four years before he came to Sul Ross, Dr. Morgan hadn't heard of me when he arrived in Alpine from the University of Missouri. That was probably a good thing, since I had received a second chance in 2007 to make a first impression.

In 1986 Dr. Morgan moved to the president's office as executive assistant and served as acting president from 1989 until his appointment as president in 1990. His hobbies included motorcycling, golf, shooting sports, classical music, and travel. At the time of our meeting, Dr. Morgan and his wife had been married forty years—five years longer than Eileen and I.

Dr. Morgan casually talked to me about our athletics budget and all that was needed for the athletics department. The school had a $12 million endowment, with only $156,000 budgeted for football. That's a month's salary for many prominent Division I football coaches.

In addition to head coach Steve Wright, we had only one other full-time football coach in assistant coach Drew Bridges. The other coaches were either graduate assistants or volunteers, or had part-time duties elsewhere at the university.

Division III schools such as Sul Ross, of course, don't offer athletic scholarships. Football is viewed as an extracurricular activity for students, and we as players paid to play a sport we loved. As a public university, however, Sul Ross offered the best deal compared to the private institutions that dominated the American Southwest Conference. Tuition and fees at Sul Ross were $4,336 in 2007; that number was $17,760 at Mary Hardin-Baylor.

But one of the things that struck me when I came back to Sul Ross was how beautiful the campus was compared to when I first attended. It was amazing, and probably one of the most beautiful small-college campuses I had ever been on. Jackson Stadium, on the other hand, was equally amazing in the other direction. The stadium was virtually the same as it had been when I'd last played. Fletcher Hall, which was the football dorm where I had lived during the 1969–70 school year, was no longer. It had burned to the ground several years after I left.

One thing Dr. Morgan and I discussed was the lack of a capital campaign, which was badly needed to supply the athletes at Sul Ross with the items needed to be competitive in the nine-team American Southwest Conference. Dr. Morgan promised me he was doing everything in his power to see that something would be put in place, sooner rather than later. He also told me he had ordered new sweats for practice before the cold weather arrived, and was working with the alumni on funding for other necessary items.

Needless to say, that was a step in the right direction.

Our opening game was successful, and it marked the first time in my football career I had missed a game because of an injury. I had no idea things would get worse before they got better.

We beat Texas Lutheran 33-31; we basically gave them four touchdowns. Quarterback Austin Davidson had a huge game. He threw for 454 yards and four touchdowns, and our offense finished with 604 total yards. Receiver Joc Quise Brown had ten receptions for 256 yards and three scores.

We outplayed Texas Lutheran, but we needed Mike Van Wagner's 26-yard field goal midway in the fourth quarter to win the game. The game was far too close for comfort, and I knew we had to play better—and I knew we could play better. That was how connected I felt with these young men.

In fact, before the team left for Texas Lutheran, I asked Coach Wright if I could speak to them. Initially Coach hesitated, and then he reluctantly agreed. He asked what I wanted to talk about. I told him I just wanted to speak about believing in themselves and let them know how I felt about them and their abilities. He told me he would not be there at the team meeting before they left for Texas Lutheran, but he would tell Coach Bridges to allow me to talk to the team.

Once at the meeting I mentioned to Coach Bridges that Coach Wright had agreed to allow me to address the guys before they left for the game. Coach Bridges told me I could speak to the team but that Coach Wright had said to give me three minutes, no more. Coach Bridges would be timing me with his watch.

I was caught off guard and wondered what that was about, but I felt I needed to take the three minutes and at least tell the players part of what I wanted to say. I was more determined than ever to let them know how I felt about them.

"I want you guys to understand what you have as a team," I told them. "I'm not blowing smoke at you; I'm not patronizing you. I've been out there with you day in and day out, and you guys have talent. You guys can play. I've been around some good programs, but I've never been around a bunch of young men as committed to giving their best each day like you are.

"I am amazed at your work ethic and your commitment to each other. You are doing more with fewer resources than any other team I have been associated with as a player or a coach. I am honored beyond words to be your teammate, and I'm impressed with your talent and self-sacrifice for each other. I want you to know I believe in you. I have no doubt about your abilities and what you can do. I just needed for you to know that and to tell you to believe in each other. Everything else will take care of itself."

It was important to me for them to know how I felt. After the game I really wanted to share in the victory with the guys, so I got up at four in the morning on Sunday and met them as they arrived back at Jackson Field. My teammates were surprised to see me, but I noticed that many yawns turned into smiles as I congratulated them.

––––––––

Coach Wright and I had mutually agreed that I would not speak with the media the first month I was on campus. He had told everyone who was interested that we would have a "media day" on Monday, September 3. As it turned out, it was a national media event and there were representatives there from ABC, *Good Morning America*, the *NBC Nightly News*, KMID-TV in Odessa, and several other local and area television and radio stations.

Dr. Morgan opened the session and introduced Coach Wright. Coach Wright talked about Sul Ross and our program for a few minutes, and then he began to discuss me as an "unusual situation" that had generated all of this attention. He said that he didn't run "Football 101" at Sul Ross and liked to believe that he was open-minded to anything that made sense. He also talked about his general approach to life as a result of having raised a daughter who had been challenged most of her life by an undiagnosed autoimmune deficiency. This had created in him a passion for those individuals and causes that were discriminated against for one reason or another—whether it was because they were female, or a minority, or handicapped, or too old.

"This is part of the reason why Mike Flynt is here. I don't do things exactly the way everybody says I ought to."

Finally, Coach Wright introduced me, and I was able to talk to the media and field questions about playing again after thirty-seven years. All the reporters were very attentive and respectful. The whole experience was extremely positive and one I enjoyed immensely.

NBC stayed and filmed me at practice. They had some questions for me about my injuries, and the reporter tried to pin me down on when I would be able to play. I responded the same way to that question each time it was asked—"That is totally Coach Wright's decision"—although I knew it would be a while longer considering my injuries. In addition to my groin strain, my neck and right shoulder had bothered me since I'd made that tackle in drills during two-a-days. I thought I had suffered a pinched nerve, but I still practiced. I didn't want to miss any time.

Our trainer, "Doc" Prude, had introduced me to some quality physical therapists in Odessa at PhyTex Rehabilitation & Sports Medicine Associates. They had a state-of-the-art laser wand that was accomplishing some amazing things to promote tissue healing. I drove 160 miles to Odessa the next day to meet with Jim Carlson, a therapist and their administrator. He was able to give me a laser treatment on my groin injury and get me back on the road to Alpine in time to make it to practice.

Practice went very well. I was in full pads and able to go through all the drills with only minor pain in my groin. My neck and shoulder felt okay too. When we lined up after practice for gears—sprints where you accelerate and then slow down—I told my teammates, especially some of the fastest players, that I could outrun them. They just laughed. I told them, "All right, just be ready and don't be surprised when you look up and I'm way out in front of you on these sprints." They were saying, "Okay, Mike, whatever you say." I told them again, "You go ahead and laugh now, but I'm going to beat you."

Well, on the tenth and final gear, I took off about two seconds before Coach blew the whistle for us all to run. I heard the guys hollering from behind me,

"Mike, you're cheating!" When we finished I turned around and held my arms open and said, "See, I told you I could beat you; that wasn't so tough!" They all thought it was pretty cool and finally, after much persuasion, conceded I had won even though I left a little early. There were congratulatory high-fives and hugs. Even as I write about this now, it still makes me smile; what a great group of guys I was fortunate enough to have as teammates.

I have always been a fan of time-travel movies—*Back to the Future* and all the sequels; *Somewhere in Time* is another favorite of mine. For me, each day at Sul Ross was like stepping back in time. I was back on the same practice field I had played on nearly forty years before; little had changed. I was suited up in full gear just like all my teammates, doing everything these nineteen-, twenty- and twenty-one-year-olds were doing, and there were no mirrors for me to look in and see the difference in our ages.

Every day I hung on to every second, because I knew this gift of time travel would end soon, and this time it would really be over for good.

On Wednesday morning I met with Dr. Morgan, Coach Wright, and representatives from the William Morris Agency, which represented clients in all segments of the entertainment industry. I had been bombarded by book and movie requests since news of my return to college football was made public. I had no idea that coming back to play football would create the national interest that it had. Eileen and I were amazed at the country's interest in what I was doing, and it seemed to escalate daily.

I was informed by the school attorney at this meeting that when I enrolled at Sul Ross, the university actually owned my rights. Essentially, as long as I was a student, I was "public domain" to the university; they could sign a book and movie deal about my life, and there was nothing I could do about it.

The William Morris Agency had three representatives there at the meeting and had a conference call set up with two more representatives—one in New York and one in Los Angeles. We watched a very impressive movie clip about William Morris and its long and storied history. They then proceeded to try and convince us to sign a deal right then because of a pending writers' strike that would slow the process down indefinitely.

I felt very uncomfortable with this whole process. I hadn't even had time to think about a book or movie, if that were to happen. This was so out of my realm of experience. And the thought that Sul Ross could sign a deal without my consent was very unsettling.

I met privately with Dr. Morgan and explained my concern, now that I had been made aware that I was "public domain"—that someone could make a movie of my life or write a book about my return to football without even getting my input. We discussed the different possibilities and both agreed that the best course of action would be to do nothing now and wait until the end of the season and see if there was still even any interest at that time.

I informed Coach Wright of our discussion, and he was in agreement also. Coach Wright told me he knew why I had come back—to play football—and it wasn't to make a movie. He also told me he had a football team to run and he trusted my judgment in that area. Those decisions were up to me.

All this talk about a book and possible movie only added to my frustration about not being able to play and make a contribution on the field. The pressure for me to play mounted each day, but I knew for me to run full speed or to make a quick direction change—plant my foot and crossover—could be a disaster for me physically. I had to be patient and allow my body to heal.

If I pushed it and tried to go too early and tore the tendon away from the bone, then I would not only be out for the season, but I would jeopardize my future health. On the flip side, if I sat out the first few games, allowed my body to heal, played, and made a contribution later in the season, then maybe everyone would forget about my injuries and the games missed. That seemed to be my best strategy.

———

Since I couldn't play yet, Coach Wright told me I wasn't on the travel squad for our second game against Southwestern Assemblies of God University in Waxahachie, Texas. I met the team at the stadium on Friday morning and wished them luck. Later that morning Eileen and I jumped into our truck and drove to the Big Bend, one of the most beautiful spots in the world. It's named for the Big Bend National Park, the westernmost region of Texas.

Eileen had listened to me for years as I told her of the crazy things I did when I attended Sul Ross. This was the first opportunity I had to actually show her the spot where one of those stories had happened. We drove about eighty miles into the Big Bend, worked our way around the sharp curves and up the steep terrain, and there it was—a rock formation off to the side of the highway that was aptly named "Rabbit Ears." It was a gradual slope up several hundred feet to two sheer columns of rocks that were almost identical, and rose another few hundred feet above the slope, straight up.

Well, one sunny day back in the spring of 1970, some teammates of mine—Ronnie Bell, Glen McWhorter, Bill Roberts, Randy Wilson, and Roel Maldonado—and I made a day trip to the Big Bend and wound up at this very spot. There was no rhyme or reason as to why we parked our car and climbed the Rabbit Ears, but we did. I am sure it had something to do with the amount of cold beer we had consumed during the drive, but who knows. The climb was fun, and most of the guys were content to walk up the slope and enjoy the scenery, thankful for an opportunity to get out of the car on such a beautiful day.

Ronnie and I had decided to see if we could climb all the way up to the "ears" and get a better view of the landscape. We realized when we reached that point that there was a huge section of rock, maybe twenty or thirty feet high and forty to fifty feet in circumference. It was about the size of a minivan, and it was separated by only a few feet from one of the ears. As we stood and looked at this boulder, I noticed that Ronnie had this all-too-familiar "mischievous little kid" grin on his face. Every time he had that look, we got into trouble.

He scrambled the rest of the way up the hill and wedged himself between the two rocks. He placed his back against one of the ears and his feet against the boulder. When I realized what he wanted to do, I said, "Ronnie, man, there ain't no way you're gonna shove that rock down; it is way too big."

He said, "You're right; I'm not if you don't help me." Never one to turn down a challenge, I quickly climbed up beside him. We realized pretty quickly that the task was going to be impossible from where we were, but as we looked at the boulder and how close it was to the ear all the way to the top, we thought *leverage*. We repositioned ourselves as high up as we could and then put our backs into the task. Just as we were about to give up, we heard rocks falling below us. Ronnie looked at me and grinned. "We moved it!" he said. "Keep pushing. Don't lose the ground we've gained!"

Now, if you've never been in the mountainous desert, then you can't appreciate how quiet it can be and how even the faintest sound will carry for long distances. While Ronnie and I worked our way up between the rocks to get in better position, we listened to the conversation between Randy, Glen, Bill, and Roel down below as they watched us. Their conversation went something like this:

RANDY: "What do you think they're doing?"

ROEL: "I don't know, but I think they're trying to shove that huge rock down this hill."

GLEN: "I think they've had too much to drink."

BILL: "What the hell are they going to do if they push that rock off and they have nothing to hold on to?"

ROEL: "I ain't worried about that; those guys are crazy and both of them are like goats. Besides, there is no way they can move that rock."

RANDY: "I'm glad I grabbed an extra beer; it's hotter than hell out here."

BILL: "What are you talking about? That's my beer; you didn't carry that out here—I did."

Randy weighed about 250 pounds at that time, and Roel about 230. Glen and Bill were both wide receivers and pretty quick on their feet, but Randy and Roel were not speed merchants. Even though they were directly in the path the boulder would take, should we succeed in dislodging it from where it had been since the beginning of time, they were not the least bit worried—yet. We kept shoving, pushing, and straining.

Then the unbelievable happened. Rocks started falling quickly below us in greater numbers, and the boulder started to move away from us. I told Ronnie we were going to need to jump to our left when it started to go to avoid the sheer drop that would be created when the boulder fell. One final push, we jumped, and the fun started.

Randy, Roel, Bill, and Glen couldn't believe their eyes. They were standing down the slope about two hundred yards, and this giant boulder was now barreling down the hill directly at them. Most of their graphic comments will not be included in this telling of the story. Suffice it to say that every curse word known to man (in English and Spanish) was screamed multiple times over the next few seconds. More bad things were said about my mother that day than I care to remember.

Glen and Bill did the smart thing and ran up the hill and around the boulder. They were out of harm's way in no time. Randy and Roel, each trying not to spill their beer, were gingerly picking their way through the cacti. Randy went left down the hill, and Roel went to the right, both feeling pretty good about their decisions. The boulder gathered speed, absolutely destroying everything in its path, crushing smaller rocks and giant cactus plants. Then, incredibly, it hit a dip in the side of the hill and split in half.

About this time Randy and Roel both looked back and, to their horror, one-half of the boulder went after Randy and the other after Roel. Beer cans were flying now, and so were the fat boys. It seemed the boulders had minds of their own and it was an all-out footrace, through the cacti and volcanic rock, all the way down the hill.

By the time Ronnie, Glen, Bill, and I got down the hill and to the car, Randy and Roel had made it safely back, though they both looked like they had run through a barbed-wire fence on the way down. They had gotten another beer and were picking cactus needles out of each other, convinced that Ronnie and I had done that to them on purpose. Like we could have planned something that bizarre!

We all survived once again, and it became another one of those stories that just gets better with the telling.

Eileen and I traveled on to Terlingua, home of the world-famous chili cook-off, passed through Lajitas, and continued on to the Rio Grande River on the Texas-Mexico border. It is very desolate yet beautiful country, and I had forgotten how hot it got there. Eileen said the wind felt like a hair dryer blowing in her face.

After some searching, we located an old abandoned house on a cliff that overlooked the Rio Grande. I couldn't believe I had found my way back to the "Rock House." I showed Eileen the spot of many great parties in college. The house was built on a rock shelf that protruded just far enough out over the river that you could dive about twenty feet into the Rio Grande, which I had done numerous times. It always felt so refreshing on a hot day in southern Texas. I did not, however, attempt that feat this time!

Although Eileen and I didn't actually cross the river into Mexico, it was routine procedure to be stopped by the Texas Border Patrol on the return from the Big Bend. One of the officers asked me where we were headed, and I told him Alpine. He asked if Alpine was home. I answered that it was my temporary home because I was in school at Sul Ross. He then asked, "Where is home?" and I told him Franklin, Tennessee.

He said, "You're the guy? You're the football player, aren't you?"

I said, "Yes, sir, I am."

He went on to say, "Man, I have been hearing so much about you, and I'm really glad to meet you." We shook hands, and he said, "I think what you're doing is great. How is your leg?"

I told him I felt better and I really hated that I didn't make the trip with the team this weekend. I noticed his name tag read "Andrews," and I told Officer Andrews I appreciated his kind words.

He said, "You are welcome; I'll be watching for you to play." I told him I hoped that would be soon.

While I wasn't able to watch or listen to our game on Saturday, we won easily, 39-7, and improved our record to 2-0. Our All-Conference running back, T. J. Barber, ran for 114 yards and was once again on track for another 1,000-yard season.

––––––––––––

The calls from the media continued to come in on a regular basis. Coach Wright wanted me to talk to the press when time allowed. He now permitted filming by the television stations and would call me to come in for radio interviews that he approved. The only shows I was able to appear on live were FOX News and *Jim Rome Is Burning,* as they sent satellite trucks to Alpine to film me. Otherwise, although I was grateful for the interest, I just wasn't able to leave and travel anywhere because I would miss football practice—something I had never done in my life.

Practices went well for me as we prepared for our third consecutive road game to open the season at powerhouse Mary Hardin-Baylor, which was ranked third nationally in Division III. I practiced at linebacker and enjoyed the contact and hitting. During our Tuesday practice I made a hard, head-on-the-numbers tackle. I had a sudden, sharp pain in my neck and right shoulder and lost all strength in my right arm, chest, and lat on my right side. I hoped the pain would go away quickly, but it did not. In fact, it only got worse. The pain was something I had never experienced before, and the lack of strength in my arm really concerned me.

I talked with Doc Prude, our trainer. He asked me to stand still as he put both his hands on top of my helmet and pushed straight down. I thought I was going to drop to my knees; the pain, right between my shoulders, was unbearable. Doc told me that it wasn't a pinched nerve as I had initially thought, but something much more serious. It was my spine. He was concerned and wanted me to see an orthopedist in Odessa as soon as possible.

He told me, "Mike, this may be over."

I said, "No, Doc, it can't be over."

I was up early on Wednesday and made the 160-mile trip to Odessa. This really wasn't a huge inconvenience, as the speed limits in that part of West Texas are seventy-five and eighty miles an hour. The roads are pretty straight and flat for the most part, and there's not much traffic in the wide-open spaces out there.

In Odessa I met with an orthopedist by the name of Dr. Richard Duke. He was gracious enough to work me into his busy appointment schedule and take X-rays of my spine. As I waited on the results, a gentleman who worked with Dr. Duke approached me and introduced himself as Johnny Gentry. He said he had followed my comeback and asked me if I remembered two very fast guys at Permian named Billy Rodgers and Jody Coleman. I told him I did, and that those guys were friends of mine. He said he went to Ector High back in the day, but those two guys were his running buddies. He said, "We were fast back then; we could turn out the light and get in bed before it got dark." We had a great time visiting while I waited on Dr. Duke.

Dr. Duke called me into his office and had good news. He showed me the X-rays and said my spine didn't look that bad. I had some arthritis in my spine but nothing that wasn't pretty normal—for a fifty-nine-year-old line-backer. Still, he wanted me to have a magnetic resonance imaging test (MRI) done on my neck at West Texas Imaging, which would give the physicians a detailed view of my spine and help them to make a more accurate diagnosis. They got me in that same day and said the results would be e-mailed to Dr. Duke as soon as they were complete.

I was back in Alpine in time for practice, but our trainer pulled me aside and said Dr. Duke had telephoned. The news wasn't good. The results of the MRI showed I had two bulged disks in my neck (C6 and C7), and if they ruptured, it could damage my spine and even cause paralysis. I was told to not even wear my helmet to jog, much less practice. My spine injury had come about a week after Kevin Everett, the twenty-five-year-old professional football player for the Buffalo Bills, had injured his spine and was carried off the field on a stretcher. I certainly didn't want that to happen to me.

My children always called to check on me and offer their encouragement. When they found out about my neck injury, they were extremely troubled.

Delanie telephoned, and she was crying. She said that I had made the team and that I had nothing else to prove. "Please come home now," she said.

Micah called and said, "Dad, this has been a wonderful, feel-good story. If you wind up in a wheelchair because of this, then it becomes a nightmare. Why don't you just stop here and not risk your health anymore?" Lily called Eileen and asked her mother to make sure I didn't do anything to risk further injury. Eileen was more than a little worried.

I explained to my family that this was something I had to do. I was confident my body would heal, and my faith in the reason I was here was strong. Somehow, I knew I would be fine.

Coach Wright had already told me that regardless of the outcome of the visit to Dr. Duke, I was on the travel roster against Mary Hardin-Baylor. He felt the team would play better if I was there offering encouragement. But he confided in me that he didn't really believe we had a chance against Mary Hardin-Baylor. He said they had an exceptional team.

We also decided we would not talk to the media or tell them the extent of my physical condition. It was a day filled with good news and bad news. I opted to focus on the good news. I was excited I was traveling with the team.

I loaded on the bus with my teammates early Friday morning for my first road trip in thirty-seven years. Coach Wright and I talked, and he repeated— even though I would be in uniform for the game—he didn't want the media to know about my neck injury. I agreed. When the media or anyone asked, the story line was that I was held out of the game because of groin and shoulder soreness.

We had to leave Alpine early Friday for Belton, Texas. Eileen drove me to the stadium at 7:00 a.m., and we sat in the truck for a few minutes, laughing at my sleepy teammates getting on their respective buses. They each had their own sleeping gear, pillow, and assortment of junk food. I knew this was going to be another great experience.

The bus ride was much different than what I remembered. For starters, the bus was far more comfortable than the ones we rode in 1969 and 1970. Second, the technology that was available on the buses was impressive—and loud. The televisions and DVD players blared wide open and nonstop. It was more of a carnival atmosphere than any previous road trip I had ever been on. What amazed me was that my teammates slept through the noise like it wasn't there. I could no more sleep on that bus than I could fly. I guess that's one of the many blessings of youth—being able to sleep through anything!

We arrived in Belton, and as we unloaded off the bus at the motel, the coaches handed out our room keys. There were three or four players to a room, and I was going to be bunking with linebackers Jarrett Ballew and Baltazar Haro. As we settled into our room, Jarrett and Baltazar told me they had met an old guy on campus who said he remembered me from back when. He had told them about a big, tough guy, a real troublemaker, whom I had whipped years ago there at the Mountainside Dorm.

"Mike," they asked me, "was that true? What was he talking about?"

I laughed and told them yes, it was true, and it was one of those strange things that just seemed to happen to me back then. I explained how a guy named Johnny had been drinking pretty heavily that day and had decided to take over the switchboard operator's duties at the dorm. He wouldn't allow any calls to come in or go out unless he knew who was on the other end. I was trying to telephone a girl at Mountainside and kept getting Johnny on the phone. After four failed attempts to get past him, I decided to pay him a visit.

When I walked in the dorm, Johnny was still there. I called out his name, and when he stood up I understood why he had been able to win a tamale-eating contest a few months earlier. He had eaten sixty-six at one sitting; this guy was big! I told him to come outside, then turned around and walked out the door. He followed me out and we fought. The fight didn't last but a few minutes, but it sure attracted a lot of attention. Word spreads fast at a small college.

The really amazing news about that particular altercation was that it got me a B in a Human Relations class. (How's that for irony?) I explained how a couple of days after the fight I ran into my professor at a local grocery store and he asked me if it was true I had whipped Johnny. I stood there and thought, *Oh, no, where is this going?* I then said, "Yes, sir, it's true."

He said, "You just made a B in my class; I can't stand that big bully, and I'm glad someone finally kicked his rear."

He was true to his word. When I went into class for the final exam, he took my paper, marked a big red B on it, and tossed it in his drawer. And believe me, I was proud of that B. Jarrett and Baltazar thought that story was pretty funny, but I also emphasized to them how God had changed a lot of things in my life since those days.

We heard the coaches in the hall banging on doors; it was time to go down to the field and begin our Friday pregame walk-through.

We rode the buses to the stadium. It was about four in the afternoon, and to say that the heat was oppressive was an understatement. We later learned that the actual temperature on the shag Astroturf was almost 140 degrees. We walked out on the field, went through our normal stretching and warm-up routine, and then ran through our kicking game coverage again and again. We started to sweat through our T-shirts, and everyone was asking for water. We were told Coach Wright had said to leave it on the bus. I looked for Coach and saw him in the far end zone talking with one of the Mary Hardin-Baylor coaches.

I told Doc, "If we don't get these guys some water and quick, we are going to have some real problems tomorrow, because they will never be able to hydrate in time for the one o'clock game." Doc sent a couple of runners to the bus, and they hauled back bottled water, but by that time it was too little too late.

———————

The day was September 15, 2007. As I ran onto the field, I realized that this was the first time in thirty-seven years I had been on the sidelines as a football player. I had been there many times as a coach at Nebraska, Oregon, and Texas A&M, but it's just not the same. My excitement was short-lived as Mary Hardin-Baylor returned the opening kickoff for a touchdown.

We were crushed by Mary Hardin-Baylor, 55-14. The temperature was well into the nineties, and we were not accustomed to the high humidity. My concerns about our lack of hydration the day before were realized more quickly, and the effects were much worse than I had feared. Our players began to cramp on the sidelines. Some of the players vomited and suffered from heat exhaustion.

To top it all off, I started looking around at our coaching staff, and they were all there on the sidelines. I asked one of the graduate assistants, Coach Allen, "Who do we have upstairs in the booth?"

Coach Allen replied, "We don't."

I said, "You're kidding me, right?"

He said, "No, Coach Wright won't put anyone in the booth." I stood there shaking my head, thinking this had to be a financial issue. Why else would he not have a coach in the booth?

We were terribly disorganized, and due to our limited coaching staff, we had very little communication on the sidelines. Coach Wayne Schroeder, the defensive line and special teams coach, did everything he could. He was running up and down the sidelines looking for replacements on special teams and defense. Our players were exhausted. Mary Hardin-Baylor lined up every play and wore us out. They had great depth at every position and rotated their players.

I was frustrated for my teammates. They never quit. They gave a valiant effort, but the heat and cramps took a brutal toll on us. Some of the players cramped so badly after the game that they couldn't remove their uniforms.

All during the game fans chanted, "Put number 49 in the game," and "Put Flynt in." Even the Mary Hardin-Baylor band got into the act and was shouting, "We want Mike! We want Mike!"

I wanted desperately to get on the field and make a contribution to my team, but Coach Wright had already told me to not even think about it. I was injured and couldn't play, and that's all there was to it.

After the game I was amazed by the response I received from the Mary Hardin-Baylor team. The players and coaches went out of their way to congratulate me and offered kind and encouraging words. It was almost like I recommitted myself because of all the positive things they had to say. I knew I was going to heal. I was going to get better.

Eileen was at all of the games, and she was my first call after practices. She knows me better than anyone, and she knew I was hurting for my teammates that day. Eileen always makes the best of things and quickly told me about the baby boomers and former teammates who had attended the game. I needed to stay positive for them, as well as for my family. We took lots of pictures with past Permian and Sul Ross teammates and their families. I knew I needed to enjoy every second of this experience.

Jaime Aron of the Associated Press also attended the game. He said he was going to start a weekly journal about me because of the amount of interest in what I was doing. He then told me he had come up with a name for me.

I said, "Oh yeah, what's that?"

"The Senior," he said.

I thought about it for a second and couldn't help but smile. I told him the abbreviation for senior was SR. That was the registered brand for Sul Ross.

"The Senior" just seemed to fit.

ELEVEN THE PRESSURE BUILDS

I didn't want to second-guess Coach Wright's decisions or game plan, but I had to be honest with him. That's why we met after the Mary Hardin-Baylor game.

I told him I didn't see how we could make the necessary adjustments that we needed to make during a game without a coach in the press box. Coaches just cannot see the entire field from the sidelines. They need a higher vantage point to get the big picture. I thought initially it was a financial issue and we weren't able to afford headphones, but I found out later that we had headphones; Coach Wright simply elected to not use them.

He never did give me a direct answer about not having a coach in the press box. I let it go. I figured he had his reasons and he wasn't obligated to tell me, but not having a coach in the press box almost cost us a crucial game later in the season.

Coach Wright didn't have a great win-loss record in his first four seasons at Sul Ross, but he proved he could win. He'd been voted Co–Coach of the Year in the American Southwest Conference a year earlier in 2006 after he guided the Lobos to a 5-4 record. It was our first winning season in ten years. Coach Wright modestly told me when we first met that one of the main reasons he was given that honor was not so much because of the win-loss record but because of what he had been able to accomplish given the lack of resources he had to work with. It was a noteworthy accomplishment.

At one point in his first three years at Sul Ross, he was 0-26. When he told me that, I tried to imagine what it must have been like going to practice each day, coaching these young men and staying in a positive frame of mind. How do you recruit with that kind of record? To me it said a great deal about the man, his commitment, and his determination to build a winning program. But I just didn't feel he was prepared to handle the outside pressure and media attention that came with me making the team at Sul Ross.

Coach Wright also had some challenges he dealt with concerning his family. His wife had just recently accepted a position at a university in Wisconsin as a grant proposal writer, and she and his daughters had moved from Alpine. When I heard about this, I thought it was a temporary situation, but then I was told by one of the assistant coaches that it was a permanent arrangement. I assume that this, too, must have been difficult for him to deal with.

Coach talked frequently about the budget and how he had only two full-time coaches on staff—himself and Coach Bridges. The others were being paid by the university in some other capacity and volunteered their time as football coaches or were graduate assistants helping out as they worked on their master's degrees.

Most of the schools in our conference were private and, like Texas Lutheran University, charged upwards of $20,000 for tuition. This gave them a much larger budget for their athletic departments. Some of the programs we faced had as many as fifteen full-time coaches. In contrast, my enrollment fee at Sul Ross for one semester as a full-time student was a little less than $5,000, and that included a $1,500 charge for out-of-state tuition.

Our first home game of the season against East Texas Baptist University on September 22 was welcomed with great anticipation. We had been on the road for three straight weeks, and it felt great to have the opposing team travel to us. Kickoff was scheduled for three thirty in the afternoon, and I had been told by several former teammates who planned to attend that every hotel and motel in the area was sold out. People had to stay as far away as sixty-seven miles in Fort Stockton. I told my teammates we were going to play in front of a sell-out crowd and that the atmosphere would be great.

Our much-anticipated home opener was a disaster. The game started nearly ninety minutes late due to rain and lightning, and it only got worse.

I kept waiting for one of the coaches to call us together for a pregame talk. We, like any team that prepares for an athletic contest, needed to hear words of encouragement. Those words help athletes of any age focus on their responsibilities and maximize their performance. Coach Wright had not allowed me to speak to the team without his permission, and I had not asked because I assumed one of the coaches would step up and make that speech. It was our home opener, and we were going to be playing in front of a huge crowd.

The speech didn't happen.

We were down 7-0 in the first quarter, but we rallied back and led 21-7 early in the second quarter. We then started to self-destruct. ETBU scored twenty-one unanswered points, and we went into the locker room for halftime down 28-21. Coach Wright stormed in and told all the trainers and coaches to get out. He then told us we quit. He said, "I saw it in your eyes at the beginning of the second quarter; you just quit on me, and I'm going to leave you here and let you figure this out on your own!"

I personally believe that Coach knew exactly what I would do when he walked out the door, and that may have been part of his plan—I don't know. But I couldn't get to my feet fast enough when he closed that door.

I shouted for the players to listen to me. I pointed at the closed door and told them that no one in that room had quit, that the only person who had quit just walked out that door. I told them Coach was wrong and didn't know what he was talking about. I told them to look around—look at each other in this room—this is who they were playing for. I told them the fans would quit on them, and the coaches had already quit on them, but we would never quit on each other. I continued: "We are the ones we play for; we are the ones making the sacrifices day in and day out. We have to believe in each other." I told them how important it was to never criticize their teammates when they made a mistake, because no one felt worse than they did when that happened.

The guys needed to know that when they made a mistake we were going to embrace them when they came to the sideline, and we were going to overcome that mistake together, as a team. I told them we were only down seven points and we could win this football game; we just needed to stay focused. We needed to have a total team commitment. Then I asked them, "Have you ever had someone spit in your face?" I told them I had. When somebody spits in your face, everything else just goes away; you have total focus and you can't think about anything else but getting your hands on that individual and kicking his butt!

"Now we have just had twenty-eight points spit in our face. What are we going to do about it?"

We came out and played our hearts out the second half, but we could not overcome the poor field position the coaches put our defense in and the momentum that ETBU had generated in the second quarter. We lost 41-28, and we gave them twenty-eight of those points. Our record dropped to 2-2 overall and 0-2 in the conference.

Coach Wright later told us, "When someone asks you what happened in this game, you tell them Coach Wright lost this game. This was the worst performance I have ever given as a head coach. I blew it. I let this team down. I let our school, our alumni, and our community down with poor coaching decisions. This is my loss and my fault." Coach Wright also said he may have cost us a chance at the playoffs because he lost this game. He said we had practice on Sunday, and he added that if we didn't beat Howard Payne the following week, he would not continue to coach at Sul Ross. He said he'd resign if we didn't win.

––––––––––

Despite the loss, many fans were impressed with our players. Some of my former teammates who had been in the coaching profession for years told me we had as good a group of skill players as any team in the conference, if not better than most. These were comments I later shared with my teammates, because they needed to hear these things. I was more than glad to tell them anything positive I could about their performance.

The pressure on me to play increased. It wasn't intentional pressure, but more in the form of support and questions about my health and when I was going to be ready. I had never been hurt before, and I wasn't used to explaining and talking about injuries.

After every game that they were unable to attend, Delanie, Micah, and Lily always called me immediately after it ended to find out how things went, how I was doing, and how my teammates were doing. It was after this particular game that I shared with Micah my frustration about not being able to play. Micah immediately jumped in to offer encouragement.

"You just need to take the bull by the horns," he said. "Don't let people pressure you about playing at linebacker. You need to let people know that you've made the team and you made it at the linebacker position. You're at practice every day, going through all the drills. You are trying to help your teammates in any way you can. At fifty-nine, no one else is doing that. You are going to heal and play at some point, and until you do, enjoy every minute of this, because it will be over before you know it. Forget about all the pressure."

He laughed when I told him he had just mentored his old man.

We started our preparations for our next game at Howard Payne University on Tuesday, September 25, 2007. And it was a good day for me.

First, I had to turn in my class grades to Coach Kealoha for eligibility purposes. Well, I had A's in my three subjects—Health in the Public Schools, Seminar in Management, and History of American Sport. I told Coach K that those grades were a little different than the last time I turned them in to my football coaches here at Sul Ross. Coach K was my linebacker coach and the coach whom I had the most interaction with while at Sul Ross. He was a huge part of my football experience, and I felt fortunate to have him.

My professors had a lot to do with my good grades. I really enjoyed being a student again, and professors Wayne Sheehan and Roger Grant played a big part in that experience. Both of these gentlemen were a little older than I was but still relatively close to my age. I have had enough life experiences to recognize preparation and planning, and these guys did an excellent job.

The coursework was challenging but enjoyable. Even my younger class-mates accepted me. It was always fun to get in a "dig" with Dr. Sheehan every once in a while about his beloved Chicago Cubs. He joked with me that I might be a footnote in his course (History of American Sport) one of these days. They both encouraged me to continue my graduate work at Sul Ross, but I couldn't put my fitness business on hold for another six months.

The better news was I felt good enough that day physically to play in our scrimmage at linebacker. It was actually my first full scrimmage in thirty-seven years, and it felt great. Who ever would have thought I would be so excited about a scrimmage? I was thrilled that both my groin and neck felt much better and neither was really bothering me.

I stood on the sideline and thought about our upcoming game with Howard Payne and how my whole family would be in the stands. I felt that I needed to get some reps at linebacker. I walked up to linebacker Curtis Smithson and told him I wanted to go for a few plays, that I was feeling really good now. He was glad to let me take his spot.

My teammates noticed me on the field and immediately began hollering, "Number 49 is in the game!" and "Mike Flynt's out there!" They had heard people in the stands calling out my number and my name at the games, so they decided to jump on the bandwagon.

Scrimmaging again at linebacker was a blast. Being able to line up, read the plays as they developed, and react to the ball was so much more fun than just going through regular drills. This was competition. Every athlete thrives on competition, and age hadn't changed that for me; the absence had only served to make me appreciate it that much more.

Anytime I was with my teammates was enjoyable for me, and the weight workouts were no exception. Things in the weight room were more relaxed but still all business. One of our graduate assistants, Coach John Pond, handled all the strength and conditioning responsibilities for our team and really did a good job. Coach Bridges was also a big help in this area, but Coach Pond was the hands-on guy. At twenty-five years old and standing six feet five and 350 pounds, Coach Pond was an imposing presence. He also handled most of the offensive line duties. I have noticed over the years that the best offensive linemen are usually the ones who play with a defensive lineman's attitude, and that was Coach Pond to a tee.

My family showed up in full force at Howard Payne as planned. My eighty-two-year-old mother lived in Brownwood, and she had been announcing to her friends for weeks that I was going to be playing against Howard Payne. My children attended the game, as did all my nieces, my grandson, my sisters, and all my in-laws. Everyone showed from different parts of Texas, Tennessee, and Oklahoma wearing their "Flynt 49" T-shirts. Even my very special eighty-nine-year-old mother-in-law was there rooting for me along with many of my friends and former teammates from Permian and Sul Ross.

But as I went through routine pregame drills, I injured myself. It was a simple drill. I backpedaled and crossed from right to left, and Coach K threw me the ball. I planted, crossed over, and caught the ball. Just as I twisted to cross over one last time, I felt a pop in my lower abdominals, and my right inner thigh tightened in the same area I had injured previously.

I thought to myself, *Man, what just happened?*

I didn't say a word to anyone, but I was extremely upset. I couldn't believe it! We headed back to the locker room, and I went straight to the restroom so I could get a look at my lower abs. I saw where it had already started to bruise from the bleeding. By the time we returned to the field for the start of the game, I could barely lift my right leg because of the pain. I knew I had torn an abdominal muscle.

I turned toward the stands and made eye contact with my sisters, Gwen and Pam, and my nieces, Trisha and Carla. I just shook my head from side to side and pointed down at my leg. They knew exactly what I was saying. I had injured myself and couldn't play. They spread the word to the rest of the family. They were disappointed, but they were there to support our team as well, and they would do that whether I played or not.

I walked over to Coach Schroeder, and he turned and looked at me and said, "You need to be ready to go in when I call for you." I reluctantly told him that I hurt myself in pregame drills and couldn't run. There was no way I could play.

My family watched my teammates play, and it was an exciting game. Mike Van Wagner kicked a 36-yard field goal with less than two minutes remaining in regulation to tie the game and send it into overtime. Mike then kicked another field goal in our second overtime, and we won, 34-31.

I was proud of my teammates, and it was an important victory because it improved our record to 3-2 overall and 1-2 in the conference. While Coach Wright fulfilled his promise of a victory, his erratic behavior continued to baffle me. But he told me after the game, "Okay, it's your time now. It's time for you to play."

I assumed he was referring to our next game in two weeks at home in a rematch against Texas Lutheran. My whole family had traveled to Brownwood to watch me play, but it wasn't meant to be. I had gotten hurt, and I just had to accept that.

Another issue that upset me at the Howard Payne game was the officiating. It was without doubt the worst job of officiating I had ever seen. We had six or seven penalties against us on both sides of the line of scrimmage that were beyond belief. Then, on Monday I found out why that might have happened.

In a casual discussion with Coach Wright, he told me the officials had approached him before the game and asked to have their picture taken with me. Coach Wright defiantly told them they could not. He said, "If you want to get all my players out here and take a picture with everyone, then you'll have your picture with Mike Flynt. But if you don't want to do that, then you can't have a picture with Flynt." There was little doubt in my mind now why the officiating had been so bad in that game.

I know Coach Wright was probably doing the best he could, trying to keep me from getting all the attention and taking away from the performance of my teammates. I was in total agreement with him, but I also felt we needed to work together and take full advantage of the situation to help the program and Sul Ross.

I had never asked for or expected all the attention. In fact, I dodged the media for the first month I was in Alpine, and at times the pressure to play was unsettling. But now, since the interest had only increased, I was glad my teammates played in front of large crowds and television cameras from all the major networks. What athlete doesn't perform better in front of a crowd and enjoy all of the media attention? Hey, this was a lot of fun, and it was a game.

On Monday, October 1, I ran into Coach Wright on my way to class. He was outside the coaches' offices. Our next game was at home in two weeks against Texas Lutheran, whom we had beaten in our season opener. He called me over and told me that one of my teammates—he wouldn't say who—had approached him and wanted to know why I hadn't played yet.

He said in all the years he had coached he had never had one player come to him on behalf of another player about playing time. He said, "I think this is a high watermark for our program." He also said that we had team pictures coming up, and several of the players had asked his permission to have their picture taken with me. He asked me if that was okay. I told him he didn't need to ask and that I would do anything for my teammates. I considered it an honor.

The season was half over. We had five games left, and this was an off week for everyone but me; I had to get myself healthy.

Early the next morning Eileen and I drove the 160 miles to Odessa once again and met with Dr. Terry Unruh. He examined my lower abdomen and diagnosed it as a torn abdominal muscle. He asked how I injured myself. I said I played football at Sul Ross and I hurt it on a crossover drill. He walked over to the counter and grabbed my folder, opened it, and said, "At fifty-nine years old you're playing college football?" He told me he was qualified to diagnose and treat my abdominal tear, but I needed to see someone else about my head. He said, "Man, you are crazy!"

Eileen and I really enjoyed the open date, but then again, our entire stay in Alpine was wonderful. Outside of football and school, we did everything together. We had only one vehicle to share, and where we lived outside of town had no Internet connection or cell phone reception. We went on daily walks, and many nights we sat on the back patio in utter amazement at the stars. Unbelievable stars. With an altitude of almost a mile high and being so far from the closest big city, there was no pollution. On a cloudless night the skies were crystal clear and we could almost count the stars in the Milky Way.

Many mornings we left corn in the yard for the deer that roamed the Davis Mountains. Eileen looked out the front door one morning, and a ten-point buck stood right in front of the porch, peering inside, just waiting for his breakfast. At times we would have as many as ten or fifteen deer in the front yard eating the corn. We saw an assortment of animals during our stay in Alpine—javelina hogs, coyotes, bobcats, elk, antelope, and roadrunners. That part of Texas is truly a unique and beautiful place. I could see why so many baby boomers were choosing Sul Ross and Alpine as a location to go back to college.

Our open date was almost over, and practices were scheduled to start again in a few days. There were things Coach Wright did that for the life of me I couldn't understand, and that was a constant source of frustration for me. But he had given me a chance to try out for the team and play again. I don't know how many coaches in the nation would have done that for a fifty-nine-year-old player.

TWELVE KEEP FOLLOWING GOD

Coach Wright had traveled to California over our open date to meet with his wife and daughters. Once he returned, he called me and asked me to come to his office. He wanted to talk.

It was Monday, October 8. A few of my teammates were in and around his office, so Coach and I stepped outside into the hallway where it was quiet and we had some privacy.

He asked, "I want to know how you feel physically. Top to bottom, how are you?"

I said, "Coach, for the most part I feel good. My neck is much better, although I don't think I should hit head-on again right away. I am still concerned about sprinting full speed and reinjuring my abdominals and this groin strain. Every time I sprint it starts tightening up on me, and the therapist told me if I pull the tendon in my groin away from the bone, I am done for sure."

Coach said, "Okay, then I want you to do what you can. To begin with, you're going to go in on every extra-point and field-goal attempt. If you can get in a hitting stance, then you're going to play." I told him I could do that, and I didn't think there was anyone out there who could just flat run over me once I was in place. He said, "Okay, we're going to do that. As long as we know your injury is not a hernia, you can plan on playing." He continued, "As your ability to run improves, we will gradually work you in on special teams. I want you to play in the rest of our games if you can."

At the end of our conversation, Coach shared with me that one of the reasons he went to California was to see a medical specialist and have some tests run. He said his health was not good. I could tell while he talked that this was just another distraction he didn't need. But I also assumed he had been through enough similar situations before that he would take this in stride and ride it out. I told him I was sorry and that I would pray for him. I asked him to let me know if he needed my help in any way with the team. He nodded and said he would. I think that was the last time we ever met together privately.

Our week of preparation for Saturday's home game against Texas Lutheran went well. To say it was a special week for me is an understatement.

At Sul Ross we had a tradition in our flexibility routine during warm-ups. The starters always faced the team in front. At one practice early in the week, junior linebacker and starter Fernie Acosta reached over and grabbed me by my jersey. We traded places. He gave me his place of honor at the front of the line. I asked him, "What are you doing?" He said, "This is your place; this is where you belong. You were a captain, and you deserve to be back in front." I was grateful for Fernie, both as a teammate and as a friend.

Game day arrived, and I knew October 13, 2007, was a special day.

The media had asked me to be on the field early for interviews and pictures. After they left, Jackson Field was empty. As I walked across the field to the parking lot, I noticed a guy who sat by himself on the visitors' bench. I glanced at him but continued to walk. Then I thought, *I wonder if that is Dennis Parker, the head coach for Texas Lutheran?* I turned around and walked toward him. As I approached I asked, "Are you the man?"

He said, "Yeah, Mike, I am. How are you doing?"

I said, "I'm doing well."

"I'm glad you came over," he said. "I wanted to tell you I played semi-pro football with a Sul Ross teammate of yours, George Short." We talked for a few minutes about George and what a good player he was back in the day. And then Coach Parker added, "I am fifty-seven years old, and I can't imagine doing what you're doing. Our whole team is pulling for you, and we are all proud of you. Are you going to get to play today?"

I told him, "I think so. I think I am going to play."

We wished each other the best and parted ways.

———————

Once again none of our coaches gave a pregame talk, but I was fine with that, because I didn't think I could have been any more ready. I didn't need any words of encouragement. Delanie, my grandson, Collin, and Lily had arrived early the previous afternoon from Tennessee, and Micah and his wife, Jennifer, had gotten in late that night. My niece, Tamara, had picked up my mother from Brownwood, and they had arrived right before game time. It was a six o'clock kickoff, and the weather was perfect with no clouds and light winds. The home stands were full; families and friends, old and new, were there in abundance.

Then, after all the years of waiting and all of the praying, it finally happened.

I played!

We marched down the field and scored on our opening drive. I went in at left up-back on our extra-point attempt at the 11:08 mark in the first quarter. My responsibility was to step down and seal the gap between myself and our left end, Homer Saenz. Texas Lutheran's number 41, Billy Hardee, lined up across from me. As he got in his stance and planted his hand on the ground, he said, "Here I come, here I come!" I don't care how many times you block your teammates in practice; there's a different mind-set when you're lined up against that opposite-colored jersey. I stepped inside, made the block on Billy, and Mike Van Wagner's kick split the uprights.

I tried to act like I had done this before as I trotted back to our sideline, but it had been thirty-seven years, and it was difficult to contain the excitement. My teammates were glad I'd gotten to play, and I stole a peek into the stands to acknowledge the support of my family.

The game went back and forth, and it seemed that neither team maintained any momentum. It was a hard-fought game between two teams that didn't want to lose. The crowd, which was in excess of three thousand fans, had grown quiet, and they were probably exhausted as well. It didn't look good for us with the game winding down. We trailed 35-27 with 1:34 to go in regulation.

That's when our All-Conference running back, T. J. Barber, came up to me on the sideline and said, "Are you ready for this?"

I looked at T. J. and he had this determined look in his eyes. I said, "Yeah, I'm ready."

On the first play from scrimmage, T. J. broke a tackle at the line of scrimmage and then another in the secondary. A cornerback had the angle on him and knocked him out of bounds, preventing him from scoring. With time running out, quarterback Austin Davidson fired a touchdown pass to Jarrett Dickerson. With thirty-two seconds left, we needed two points to tie the game and send it into overtime.

Then something started to happen in the stands behind us. All we knew was that the crowd had become deafening. A few minutes earlier the fans were totally subdued. Now the crowd was on their feet and there was a constant roar of "GO, LOBOS, GO!"

Everybody at Jackson Field that day—players, coaches, and fans—knew who was going to get the ball for the two-point conversion attempt. It didn't matter. T. J. took the ball, went wide right, and would not be denied. We were all tied up, 35-35.

Texas Lutheran had the ball first in overtime. They ran three unsuccessful plays from our 25-yard line as our defense held for very short yardage. Coach Parker sent his All-American kicker, Holt Storrie, on the field for what we thought was a field-goal attempt. When they broke the huddle and lined up for the kick, three players headed to the sideline, but only two left the field. A wide receiver stayed on the field near the sideline. Had we had a coach in the press box, he would have spotted this immediately and signaled for a time-out.

But we didn't notice the receiver, and neither did our defensive backs until it was too late. Texas Lutheran lined up and faked a field goal. The quarterback rose up, stepped back, and lobbed a lazy pass into the wide receiver's hands as he walked into the end zone. They kicked the extra point, and the score was 42-35.

On our first possession in overtime, T. J. Barber once again stepped up and made an amazing short-yardage sprint for the corner, extended the ball over the goal line as he was being hit, and scored a touchdown. Mike kicked the extra point, and we were tied again, 42-42.

In the second overtime we fumbled the ball on our possession and Texas Lutheran recovered. Now they had a shot to win the game. Our defense continued to play great and held Texas Lutheran to short yardage. Once again kicker Holt Storrie was back on the field to win the game. We knew this time there would be no fake. It was going to be a 39-yard attempt, which for him was a "chip shot," and I couldn't bear to watch. I put my head down, closed my eyes, and decided to let the crowd tell me what happened. They did too. Storrie missed the field goal wide left, and the cheers were deafening.

We went into triple overtime, and Texas Lutheran had possession first. They ran a couple of plays without success and then went for it all—a pass into the end zone. One of our defensive backs, Dominique Jones, went high into the air and made an incredible interception.

Now it was our turn.

We had a couple of unsuccessful running plays, and then a holding penalty pushed us back ten yards to our 35-yard line. Things weren't looking good, but then Jamal Groover, one of our running backs, caught a pass from Austin Davidson in the left flat. He started back to the right across the field, couldn't find any running room, and then reversed his field and came back to the left. He picked up a great block from Austin, gave a supreme effort in fighting for extra yardage, and was finally tackled at midfield. We were once again in field-goal range. It was fourth down, and we had to go for the three points and the win. It was a 41-yard field-goal attempt.

As I ran onto the field for the seventh time during the game, I actually felt the difference between this time and my previous six trips on the field. The crowd was different, my teammates were different, Texas Lutheran was different, the pressure—it was so different.

I lined up next to Homer and listened to Billy once again tell me he was coming. The ball was snapped, and I blocked Billy. As soon as I looked up I heard Mike's foot hit the ball behind me. I turned my head to the right, and it seemed that everything was in slow motion. I watched the ball float, end over end, through the middle of the uprights. I knew it was good. We had won!

We had won 45-42! In triple overtime! My first game back in thirty-seven years, and we won in triple overtime!

I must have said, "Thank You, Lord," a dozen times over the next few seconds. It had been an "over and above" answer to prayer. I turned and looked for Mike to congratulate him, but he had sprinted toward the other end zone. Our whole bench unloaded and gang-tackled him on about the 20-yard line, and the celebration started. What an amazing, picture-perfect game!

The jubilant crowd spilled out of the stands and onto the field. Lily ran up to me carrying my grandson, Collin. She was so excited about me playing and the amazing win. I hugged her, grabbed Collin, and, with him in my arms, tried to congratulate everyone on our team for this incredible, special victory. It was truly a team, school, alumni, family, and community effort. Everyone played a part in helping attain the victory that day.

A television reporter came up to me after the game and asked me if this unbelievable game had completed my comeback. I responded, "No, but it's a great start!"

───────────

It was a few days later when I received an e-mail that Randy Jackson, a Sul Ross alum, had sent out to the baby boomers recounting his personal experience of what had happened during the Texas Lutheran game. To retell his story in my words would not do it justice. With Randy's permission I have included his story below. (I have taken the liberty to omit certain words so as to keep the story rated "PG.") I never get tired of reading this:

> Long story short . . . I ended up in Florida, stinkin' job getting in the way of Lobo football. I tried to hook up via the Internet, kept getting some sign about my plug-in . . . what does that mean?? Thank God perennial cheerleader Jack Cooper made the trip and as promised had a fully charged cell phone and one

on standby. For a while he sent a text message every minute or so, then he just called and decided to give me a play by play. Jack's prowess as an announcer left a little to be desired, with play calls such as "Oh, s—, that skinny kid is in again; dang it, they are going to throw it to him. . . . Oh, s—??" "Jack—Jack what's going on?" . . . Jack . . . Whewww! He overthrew him. Yet his true spirit more than made up for his other shortcomings. (Believe me, this is not an exaggeration; the night was filled with such descriptive analysis.) It all got very interesting in the fourth quarter when Jack described another "Oh s—! They intercepted it—it's a touchdown—we are down by eight. . . . Oh, well, it was a good try." . . . On the other end I'm saying, "Don't worry, Jack; we can score and go for two and get it to overtime." . . . The once-rowdy crowd had gone silent—even over the phone it was evident . . . then I heard the building chant of "GO LOBOS, GO! GO LOBOS, GO! GO LOBOS, GO!" . . . It finally got so loud I could barely hear Jack over the noise. He mumbled something about "You won't believe what is happening; they are taking over." . . . About then I heard, "Oh, s—, he caught it in the back of the end zone . . . touchdown Lobos!"

To be a little more specific about my situation, I was in the parking lot of a convenience store in Ocala, Florida. I had managed to locate one of the few cell signals in town, and I was not about to give it up. So there I was walking circles around my car, yelling into the phone . . . "YES! . . . YES!" . . . We're now in overtime. S—, they score. . . . We've got the ball . . . double s—! My battery is gone. . . . I scramble through all my stuff, move the coon dog out of his seat (he was lying on the charger), and get it hooked up again. First thing I hear, "Lobos on the 2-yard line, fourth down. This is it"—Cooper is now hoarse, the crowd is crazed, and I am on the verge of a stroke. . . . "LOBOS SCORE! . . . Oh s—, oh s—, Flynt is in again. . . . Extra point is good!" . . . Overtime two . . . Lobos have the ball first . . . nothing doing. Bad news; they have an All-American field goal kicker; doesn't look good. . . . Defense steps up; they are ready to try a 39-yard field-goal. . . . Silence. . . . Cooper screams, "Wide left! Wide left!" . . . Pandemonium! I have never heard a Lobo crowd so out of control. . . . "GO LOBOS, GO! GO LOBOS, GO! GO LOBOS, GO!" . . . Third overtime; their ball first . . . long pass . . . Jack says, "Oh s—, it's a long pass into the end zone, it is, it is, it is . . . INTERCEPTED! Oh s—, we intercepted it!". . . . Jack goes voiceless, I go numb, the crowd goes crazy . . . LOBO BALL. I pray, "Dear God, please do not let us come so far, so very far, and not reward us with a victory." . . . Back to the game . . . a sack, a loss of a couple of yards, not quite in field-goal range. We'll run one more play and try to get a little closer. . . . No luck . . . stopped us cold. Mike's back in . . . that skinny kid is gonna give it a shot. . . . About this time I have a vision of friends and fans all over the country huddled around computers, me in Florida, Randy Wilson in North Carolina, that stranger who called me from New York, those countless believers that we had recruited along the way—all hanging on every word, hope mixed with prayer that we could some way pull it off, that Mike's return would be accented by a team effort of courage and inspiration.

Jack says, "Mike's in. . . . They're ready. . . . Snap, it's down. . . . It's up . . ." Silence—silence . . . "IT'S GOOD, IT'S GOOD! LOBOS WIN, LOBOS WIN!!" . . . I can hear the crowd erupting in the background, Jack's voice is completely gone, I collapse on the hood of my truck. . . . I need a minute. . . . I call Randy Wilson; I admit there were tears. What a great moment.

Don't miss the point of all this. . . . It is not about winning a football game; it is not about a bunch of strangers who have now been welded into the best of friends; it is not even about Mike Flynt's incredible journey. What it is about is the undeniable human spirit. I will always believe that in the last minute of that game something told those kids, "This is the time for us to step up. We can do this . . . We can win . . ." And so they did.

At the first of this story, I said something about Jack saying, "You won't believe what's going on . . ." Here is what he later told me: "We were behind by eight; there were only a couple of minutes left to go; it was pretty obvious that it was over. The crowd was worn out and very quiet. . . . Then three women stood up in the front of the stands, turned to the crowd, and started yelling, "GO LOBOS GO! GO LOBOS GO! GO LOBOS GO!" It spread over the crowd like wildfire; before I knew it the whole place was standing and yelling at the top of their lungs—they just refused to quit." By the way, guess who it was who led the chant??? Not the alumni, not the students, not the cheerleaders. . . . IT WAS THE FLYNT GIRLS!!!! How about that, sports fans? Put that picture on your TV and in your newspapers; spread that one on the cover of Texas Monthly.

So in my mind that's how it ended . . . Mike Flynt making a great block—from the ground he looks up and sees the ball sail through the uprights. He's a kid again . . .

As big a thrill as Permian's '65 state championship? Probably not. . . . But then, in its own way . . . maybe so. Mike walks off the field, grandson hoisted on his shoulder, big smile . . . Four generations standing in line to share the moment. . . .

It doesn't get any better than this . . . RJ

It was months later, while cleaning out my office at home in Franklin, Tennessee, that I came across a 2007 calendar I had thrown in the trash. I had a speaking engagement scheduled, and I wanted to make sure our game against Texas Lutheran was indeed on October 13. That was a special weekend. Besides the game, Lily's nineteenth birthday was October 12 and Eileen's and my thirty-fifth anniversary was October 14.

I also noticed the bottom of the calendar from In Touch Ministries. It read:

"KEEP FOLLOWING GOD . . . YOU MAY LEARN THAT YOUR BIGGEST FAILURE WAS ONLY THE BEGINNING OF YOUR GREATEST SUCCESS!"

I had not seen that statement the whole time the calendar had hung on my wall. But I was reminded of something Eileen had told me a couple of months earlier when I had just found out from Coach Wright that I had made the team.

She said, "Isn't this so amazing, that God knew when you got kicked out of Sul Ross years ago that this day would come? He knew that we would meet, get married, have our children and our grandson, and then thirty-seven years later He would give you back that senior year that you lost."

You're right, Randy. It doesn't get any better than this.

THIRTEEN A SPECIAL HOMECOMING

We played a solid game in our 26-21 victory over McMurry University on October 20. I played four snaps on extra points, and again it felt good to make a contribution. It was our third consecutive victory, and we stood 5-2 overall and 3-2 in the American Southwest Conference. The coaches told us we had a chance to make the playoffs if we ran the table, and that was our goal.

I was really impressed by our quarterback Austin Davidson. He came out for the second half without his pads because of a bad ankle sprain. Our offense really struggled without him, and then I looked up and he had his pads back on as he hobbled back into the game. Austin threaded the needle on a pair of passes to get us to McMurry University's 3-yard line. Carlo Dominguez replaced Austin, and we scored to put the game out of reach.

Austin's commitment and the leadership he provided were qualities that I noticed in my teammates each week. Somebody always stepped up for the team, and for me it was extremely gratifying to see my teammates mature and grow as team players.

After the game I visited with Coach Larned and Coach Hensley, two of my former coaches who were big influences in my life. They each commented on my teammates and the obvious talent we had on the Sul Ross team.

As we talked I noticed number nineteen from McMurry University standing off to the side. He wanted to talk with me. We shook hands and he told me his name was Bert Green. He said, "I think we were the two oldest guys out here on the field today. I am thirty-three and I know you are fifty-nine, so I wanted to introduce myself and just let you know that I am praying for you."

I told Bert that he had made all our defensive coaches go slack-jawed at his display of speed on the field; we had changed our whole defensive game plan to cover him! Coach Larned later told me Bert was a five-time college All-American and a world class sprinter who also played professional baseball for several years before he decided to return and get his degree at McMurry University. Bert said he was a psychology major and he looked forward to receiving his degree and helping people. *And he's still accomplishing all this at thirty-three years old?* I thought. I told him I would be praying for him as well, and I've thought of him as an inspiration ever since.

———————

It was October 26, 2007.

The homecoming spirit had started to overtake Sul Ross and the city of Alpine that Friday afternoon. It started with a parade through downtown. Then the Sul Ross Baby Boomers dedicated two beautiful engraved stone benches at the Gallego Center athletic building. One bench recognized the Class of 1964 – Class of 1974, and the other one was dedicated to the "2007 Sul Ross Football Team and Mike Flynt, No. 49." The bench dedication was a wonderful gesture. It was a time for past and current football players to meet for the first time and for alumni to reconnect.

The school held a pep rally and had a bonfire Friday night. Numerous parties were planned, and traffic on the two main streets near campus, East Avenue E and East Holland Avenue, was heavy.

My former teammates from 1969 and 1970 had been arriving all day from across the Chihuahuan Desert. Many of them brought their wives or friends and family. My mother, oldest daughter, son-in-law, grandson, and one of my nieces were in town too. I was energized by the enthusiasm and participation from the locals, families, and alumni, and excited that a large crowd was expected at the game on Saturday.

We met later Friday night for a few hours at the Holland House Hotel. I hadn't seen or talked to some of my former teammates in thirty-seven years.

Others I had seen in San Antonio a few months earlier. It was really tremendous to have everyone there.

Randy Wilson, my former roommate and one of my closest friends, came up to me at one point in the evening and said, "You know, I've been reading all this stuff about you saying that you let us down and we were disappointed in you. We never blamed you. We knew what happened wasn't your fault, and you never let us down. Now look what's happened. We're all back here together again." That comment made me feel much better about everything.

I slept great Friday night. I was up early the next morning, which was normal for me, but I also knew I had to be at the stadium earlier than usual due to the pregame ceremony. I felt good, and thoughts about the game started those old familiar "game day butterflies."

Saturday, October 27, 2007, was ideal game-day weather in Alpine. It was one of those postcard-perfect snapshots; I don't think there was a cloud in the entire state of Texas. The sky was a rich, deep blue. The sun was bright and warm above the Davis Mountains.

The temperature was 70 degrees, and a slight wind blew from the northeast. A crowd of nearly four thousand fans—most of them dressed in our Lobo colors of scarlet and gray—had wedged into the Jackson Field stands and stood along the chain-link fence for our homecoming game against Hardin-Simmons University. This was a big game for us, and we had a lot riding on the outcome: a victory today would keep us on track for the playoffs and a new level for the Sul Ross program.

I was in uniform early as I made my way outside of our locker room underneath the visitors' stands at Jackson Field. My current teammates still had plenty of time and continued to dress. I nervously paced and tried to catch a glimpse of the field as the pregame ceremony, heralded with cheers and applause, had started.

It had already been an amazing two days. I was standing there with my eyes closed, trying to process this incredible experience, when our assistant coach, Coach Bridges, walked up to me. He said, "I think you have accomplished everything you came back here to accomplish, and I'm proud to say I know you." I thanked him and thought how grateful I was for his kind words, as well as the many heartfelt expressions so many people had shared with me on this journey. Their encouragement had kept me going through my injuries.

My former teammates were all lined up on the field facing the home crowd. They were going to be introduced before the game started. I listened as the announcer began to read their names over the stadium speakers. First he said what high schools they had attended, then the positions and years they played at Sul Ross, and finally their names. Lastly the stadium announcer said, "From Odessa Permian, linebacker, 1969, '70, and now 2007, number 49, Mike Flynt."

As I ran across the field from behind the stadium and through the end zone, I realized I couldn't look at my former teammates while I was running to meet them because I knew I would start crying—which I did anyway. So I looked down as I ran until I got close to them, and then, when I looked up, most of them were crying too! I went down the line and hugged every one of them. It's hard to put into words the excitement we were feeling being back there together on Jackson Field.

I couldn't help but think back briefly to the last time we'd played together on this same field. It was November 14, 1970. We were playing Southwest Texas State, and it was our final home game that season. We whipped the Cats 45-20 for our sixth victory. Our senior quarterback, Ronnie Bell, threw for 150 yards and rushed for 54 yards to set a single-season record for total offense with one game to play. Fullback Willie Dickson had 221 rushing yards and scored three times. Another memory from that day was the weather. The stands at Jackson Field were nearly empty because of frigid, freezing conditions.

Finally, as part of the pregame events, all of the current seniors were asked to come down on the field and were presented with trophies in honor of their achievements. In Division III the retention rate for a team on a year-to-year basis is about 50 percent, so to have seven seniors on a team is a noteworthy accomplishment. Milo Garza, Preston Watts, Chris Vela, T. J. Barber, Austin Davidson, Nathan Graham, and myself, along with all of our parents who were in attendance, were introduced. Each of the mothers was given roses. In my case, my eighty-two-year-old mother and my wife, Eileen, received roses.

Our school president, Dr. Morgan, then presented me with a citation from the governor of Texas that congratulated me on my return to college football. And if the past two days hadn't already been incredible enough, to top it all off, my current teammates had voted me one of four game-day captains for the coin toss. What a thrill it was to walk out on the field with them for that! We won the coin toss and elected to defer to the second half, which meant we kicked off to Hardin-Simmons to start the game.

———

As I returned to our sidelines, I noticed my mother was seated up in the stands directly behind us. She wore a gray sweatshirt that had "Mother of 49" printed across the front in red letters. I couldn't help but smile; she's been cheering for me my whole life.

Mom had watched me at another homecoming game on this field thirty-eight years before. We were hard-pressed to top that game in 1969, my sophomore year, when we upset the number one team in the nation, Texas A&I, 13-12. The celebration from that win lasted so long that the school president canceled classes the following Monday.

I thought back on that homecoming in 1969. Texas A&I was a beast. The Javelinas had lost the 1968 NAIA championship game and had won everything since; they were undefeated when they arrived in Alpine for our homecoming game. We had lost four of our first six games that season, and no one gave us much of a chance.

We watched a lot of game film on A&I, and we were pretty intimidated by the Javelinas' size and speed. As Randy Wilson and I headed to the field house to get ready for the game, he drove his car up on the railroad tracks that ran near the stadium and stopped the car. I sat there for a second, lost in thought, and then realized we weren't moving. I looked at Randy and asked him why he'd stopped on the tracks. He didn't even glance at me. He just said, "I think I would rather just sit here and wait on a train than go and play those guys." We both had a nervous laugh and then drove down to get ready for the game.

Right before we took the field for pregame warm-up, Coach Harvey told us he had walked out of the locker room and looked at the stands, which were filled with our fans. Coach then started to cry. He said he was sorry about the tears, but he just didn't want to see us get embarrassed by A&I in front of our hometown fans and alumni. It was Harvey's attempt to motivate us, and it worked. I had never seen a coach cry before, and the thought of someone embarrassing me really created an adrenaline rush, the likes of which I had never experienced in football before. I wanted to be on the field so badly I remember being furious after we won the coin toss and elected to receive. I wanted our defense on the field first so I could get out there.

Late in that game, as we protected our one-point lead, it looked as if A&I might rally for the win. The Javelinas completed a pass to our 1-yard line, but the play was whistled back due to a clipping penalty. We held them; they wouldn't get any closer. Winning that game gave me an awesome feeling. We recovered four fumbles and intercepted two passes to secure the victory.

Harvey, in a postgame interview with the *Standard Times*, called the victory "the greatest team effort ever performed by a group of boys." Harvey also told the story about how the coaching staff kidded us about being "Christians going into the lions' den." He said one of the players reminded him the Christians had a pretty good coach and ended up winning. After the game, someone—I don't know for sure who it was, maybe our quarterback, Joe Priest—wrote on the blackboard in our locker room, "Christians—13, Lions—12."

I thought about Sam Sizemore and the prediction he'd made about Texas A&I several months earlier on my first trip to Sul Ross. How wrong he had been.

That game was a long time ago, but those memories and more were reasons why the 2007 homecoming meant so much to me. I had been there before. I knew what a great feeling it was when everyone played as a team and made that "focused" attempt to accomplish the impossible, like beating the nation's top-ranked team. The difference now was that I knew we had the talent to beat Hardin-Simmons, but we were going to have to play an all-out team effort to do it.

It was a hard-fought game, very physical and emotional. Hardin-Simmons had a good football team; they were well coached, and they definitely came to play. The game was nip and tuck for nearly three quarters. Hardin-Simmons led 6-0 in the first quarter, but we tied it in the second quarter on Carlo Dominguez's 6-yard run. Both teams had missed their extra-point attempts.

Hardin-Simmons surged in front 18-6 in the second quarter on a pair of touchdown passes, but we again answered and narrowed the deficit to 18-13 at halftime on Austin Davidson's 44-yard pass to Dominguez. We captured the lead in the game when Jamal Johnson returned the opening kickoff of the second half 86 yards for a touchdown. Our two-point conversion pass attempt was incomplete, but we led 19-18 and the homecoming fans were absolutely thrilled.

Hardin-Simmons, however, scored 22 points in the third quarter; that was really the difference in the game. We managed to pull within 26-22 at the 4:07 mark in the third quarter on a 34-yard field goal by Michael Van Wagner. But the visitors quickly built a double-digit advantage and led 40-22 as we headed into the fourth quarter. Nevertheless, as I was walking the sideline, watching my teammates, I couldn't help but be impressed with their tenacity and the fact that not one player had given up. We still believed, to the man, we would win this game. I was confident and so were they.

After Hardin-Simmons scored on quarterback Justin Feaster's fifth touchdown, making it 46-29 with ten minutes left in the game, we all pulled together. Davidson's 49-yard pass to Dominguez gave us possession at the Hardin-Simmons 4-yard line. T. J. Barber rushed for three yards, and one play later, Dominguez scored his third touchdown of the game on a one-yard run. Van Wagner's extra point was good, and we trailed by ten points at 46-36.

We forced Hardin-Simmons to punt on their next possession. We regained the ball with 7:05 left in the game and moved the ball 45 yards in nine plays to the Hardin-Simmons 26. But Van Wagner's 44-yard field goal attempt was blocked, and Hardin-Simmons recovered at our 10-yard line with 4:08 remaining. We weren't finished yet.

Chris Vela recovered a Hardin-Simmons fumble at the visitors' 46-yard line with 1:39 left in the game. Davidson drove us to the Hardin-Simmons' 34-yard line, then lofted a pass across the middle to wide receiver Sean Collins. Sean made a great catch and then broke a tackle, then another. It looked like he might score as he fought with everything he had to get loose. Suddenly, the ball came out. One of the Hardin-Simmons defenders had gotten his hands on the ball and ripped it out of Sean's arms. Hardin-Simmons recovered and ran out the clock. We lost 46-36.

Sean was devastated, but I told him later that it was okay. He had given his all throughout the entire game. That's what was important—to never stop fighting to win or be satisfied with mediocrity, because when you do, mediocrity will define you.

It was a tough loss for our team, and that was difficult to accept. I was on the field for seven plays in the game. It was my third consecutive week of games, and I successfully made all of my blocks and forced the return of a blocked kick to be taken to the other side of the field. I was content to do my job and thankful to be in the game as a blocking back on field goals and extra points until my injuries healed.

Despite the defeat, everyone stayed around after the game; it was a madhouse. I was able to meet a lot of my teammates' families, as well as the Hardin-Simmons head coach, Coach Keeling, and his wife. I also met quite a few of their players, including their quarterback, Justin Feaster, who really had an outstanding game. There were pictures and congratulations all around.

It was after this game that Jaime Aron of the Associated Press spoke with Jamal Johnson, one of our defensive backs who was also from Odessa-Permian. The newspaper article the next day read: "Even though Flynt is eight years older than Coach Wright, we still consider him a peer. He's doing the same things we're doing every day, so his words mean more [than the coaches']," Johnson said. "He's a teammate for sure, to the heart," Johnson said as he banged his chest twice for emphasis. "We accepted Mike from day one. Everybody was trying to make fun of us for having this fifty-nine-year-old, but they don't know him; to us he is our teammate. Can't nobody erase that."

I can't begin to explain how I felt when I read those words. I wished everyone who loves the game of football could meet these young men personally and watch them play, and then they might understand why that statement will always be so special to me.

————————

Back on the other end of the timeline, my former teammates had gathered together after the game for pictures as well. It wasn't long before we were making fun of each other and hurling comments just as we had done in the old days. The difference this time was that the jokes were mainly about our old age and the limitations. That's when Terry Stuebing said, "Mike, we were going to carry you off the field, but we're just too dang old!"

I finally made it to the locker room and waited until all the coaches had left. I then told the players how proud I was of each one of them. As I watched them on the field and on the sidelines, I honestly thought for the first time all season that all the players had started to believe in themselves and in each other. For the first time, as a team, no one had quit out of anger or frustration, but everyone had fought to the very end, believing all along we could win. It was a superb team effort.

Later that night all the Sul Ross Baby Boomers, friends, and families had a party at the Alpine Country Club. We celebrated just being together and talked more about old times and new. We finished off the weekend with breakfast the next morning; then we all headed back to our respective homes, promising to get back together again the next year for the 2008 Sul Ross homecoming.

————————

We had two regular-season games left on our schedule—at Louisiana College in Pineville, Louisiana, and at home against Mississippi College. We now were 5-3 overall and 3-3 in the American Southwest Conference. We realized our chance to make the Division III playoffs was basically lost in our homecoming defeat, but our incentive was still to finish on a strong note.

We left late Friday afternoon by bus from Alpine for the fourteen-hour, 815-mile drive to Pineville, which is located in the middle of Louisiana. We made it to Pineville just fine, but on the way to the game the next day, the bus driver got lost and we barely got there in time for the kickoff. We didn't have time to warm up; we had just enough time to get dressed and line up for the opening kick.

Once again Eileen and some of my family members traveled to the game in Louisiana. Some of our very best friends—Skip and Janeane Decker and Ron and Dana Carter—from our church in Franklin made the two-day drive down for the game as well. They were all there to offer their support—and what a game it was. It wasn't decided until literally at the last second.

We trailed 38-24 with 4:52 remaining, but we stormed back behind a pair of Austin Davidson touchdown passes—11 yards to T. J. Barber and 28 yards to Jarrett Dickerson on the game's final play that pulled us within one point at 38-37. I lined up at left blocking back on our four extra points and a 46-yard field goal by Mike Van Wagner. As I sprinted on the field for Mike's game-tying extra-point attempt, I really believed we were headed to overtime and we would win this game. We had finished the game so impressively.

Mike kicked the extra point, and it split the uprights, but one of the Louisiana College coaches had called a time-out right before we snapped the football, so the officials took the point off the scoreboard that would have tied the game. Mike kicked the extra point again, the official paused, then ruled the ball missed wide of the left goalpost. That was on my side, and I had a perfect view. I swear the kick was good. It was close, just inside the left upright, but the kick was good. It was such a disappointing defeat because we had fought so hard and come back against overwhelming odds to put ourselves in position to win. But like so many things in life, sometimes there's just absolutely nothing you can do about what's happening, fair or not. So all we could do was return to the buses and prepare for the long journey back to Alpine.

I had an unusual request on Tuesday, November 6. I was selected by the NCAA for a random drug test. It didn't come as a surprise, because I thought there might be an issue at some point with my age, where somebody said, "This guy has to be taking growth hormones, steroids, or something. At fifty-nine, you can't do what he's doing."

I completed the drug test (a urine sample) in our training room. The NCAA tests for stimulants, street drugs, and anabolic agents, such as steroids. While the results would be forwarded to the school, I was told I would not be notified unless I tested positive for a banned substance.

I never heard a word. It was funny, because earlier in the season I joked that if I was selected, I might test positive for Geritol, the vitamin and mineral supplement that appealed to the older crowd.

Practice for our final regular season game against Mississippi College went well for me physically; I was starting to feel really great. The strength was almost completely back in my right arm, and my neck seldom bothered me. My groin still wasn't 100 percent, but I participated in our scrimmages and really believed I was well enough to contribute at linebacker for the first time since two-a-days.

Coach Wright, who missed three days of practice earlier in the week due to personal reasons, informed us we had been invited to play in the Aztec Bowl in Chihuahua City, Mexico, in December. Everyone was pretty pumped. He told us we would meet at the coaches' offices next Tuesday after the game and get our workout plans and travel agenda. This became the main topic of discussion between the players. This was really a cool deal, and we were already making plans to totally enjoy this last trip together.

As I drove home from practice on Friday, I pulled up behind the Mississippi College buses stopped at a traffic light. They had just arrived in town and were on their way to check in at the Ramada Inn. I had no idea how long the players had been on those buses, but I was hoping they were going to be worn out by game time tomorrow.

I did not get my wish. They dominated us, and we trailed 42-15 at halftime. The penalties all season long had just not been in our favor, but this was a home game, and the officiating was worse than the Howard-Payne game.

We went into the locker room at halftime, and Coach Wright was really critical of how we had played. And that was fine; we needed to fix it, but there was no time spent on adjustments. Instead, Coach Wright told us that because of our poor effort, "The Aztec Bowl is probably off."

We looked at the Aztec Bowl as our reward for a long, hard season that might have been much more successful under different circumstances. While we found out weeks later that the NCAA denied our bid to the Aztec Bowl because it was played during finals week, it was the wrong time for Coach Wright to tell us we had lost the invitation to the Aztec Bowl.

It was bittersweet for me that I completed my comeback when I played in the game's final series at linebacker.

I had hoped to play the entire season at my old position, but it didn't work out that way. Toward the end of the game, I noticed Jamal saying something to Coach Wright. I also heard my former teammate, Stan Williamson, in the stands behind us holler, "Put Mike in the game!" Stan was the guy who had challenged me at our reunion the previous summer, saying, "Why don't you?" Coach Wright jerked his head around and looked at the clock, then told Jamal, "Go find Mike!"

When Coach Wright told me last July that I could try out for his team, I thought that one of the linebacker positions would be mine. I wanted to start. That was how I had always played the game, and as far as I was concerned, this time would be no different. But it was.

I realized after my injuries slowed me down that I was grateful to have earned the right to be part of the team and contribute in some way at fifty-nine years old. We had players who were injured during two-a-days and had to miss more games than I did or were out for the entire season. I was one of the lucky ones.

Jamal found me on the sidelines, and I walked over to Coach Wright, who had just called a time-out. He asked me if I could go in at linebacker. I said, "You bet!" He asked Coach K, our linebacker coach, whom I needed to replace. I looked at Coach K and said, "Fernie."

Coach K said, "Okay, go do it."

I trotted out on the field, but I was pretty oblivious to anything around me. The first thing I did was tell Fernie I was glad it was him I was replacing. And I meant that with deep respect. Fernie had been not only a great teammate but a good friend. He hugged me and told me he was glad I finally had the opportunity to play linebacker, and better yet, he was happy I was taking his place.

I was later asked who on the 2007 Sul Ross team most reminded me of myself when I played nearly forty years ago, and I answered without hesitation, "Fernie."

For the final three minutes and thirty-nine seconds of the game, I played linebacker against Mississippi College. I was part of a gang tackle on my first play and held my ground against a six-foot-five, 270-pound guard on the second play; I forced the running back inside, and Nate Graham made the tackle. The other plays were runs away from my side; I checked my keys then pursued the plays.

And then, just like that, it was over.

We played hard in the second half, as we had in the first, but we were pretty much outcoached and outmanned. It was a predictable disaster. We had self-destructed and lost the game 56-35.

It marked the fifth straight game I had played in, but being at linebacker again was different. Travis Hendryx, our school's sports information director, told the media following the game that, "Whenever he's gone in on extra points and field goals, it drew a great reaction from the crowd, but the crowd just lit up this time. The press box did too. We've all been waiting so long for that to happen. I'm glad he was able to get in and see some action at linebacker."

Several people congratulated me after the game. One of the Mississippi College coaches mentioned to me that the big offensive lineman who blocked me was his son, Nelson Craddock. He asked if I minded having a picture taken with him and the rest of the offensive line. I told him I would love to. It was a pleasure to meet those young men and shake hands with each of them.

After the game I looked around the locker room at my teammates and thought about how grateful I was to have had the opportunity to play with this very talented and special group of guys. Sul Ross had eight players recognized for postseason honors, and Carlo Dominguez was named Freshman of the Year. My former coaches and teammates and I had been right about the amount of talent we had on our team.

This football season had been amazing—one I would never forget.

Clint Kiger, a freshman, had his locker next to mine. Clint looked at me after that last game and said, "It seems like it was just yesterday we were getting ready for two-a-days, and now it's over."

I nodded and thought to myself, *Clint, you have no idea how fast time will pass.*

FOURTEEN PAYING IT FORWARD

The painful memory of the mistakes I had made in the past was the biggest motivator inspiring me to try and make the team again, regardless of my age.

I felt that if I was able to make the Sul Ross team in 2007, I would have an opportunity, a second chance, to rewrite the ending of my story. It was never about trying to undo the past. That 1971 season and those teammates were part of history. I knew I could not explain to anyone, no more than they could explain to me, what I needed to do personally to overcome that great regret in my life. But if I were to go and try to make the team, maybe my example would give others the courage to do the same—to make an effort, take action of some kind, do something constructive, and gain the peace that would come from at least trying.

I knew once I made the team I had to be careful to walk that fine line between player and coach. I was on the team as a player and a teammate, and I always tried to keep that in my mind. It would have been inappropriate to try to take on a position of authority, but I felt it was incumbent upon me to share all I could of myself with my new teammates, both on and off the gridiron. And for me, that would be enough. That was why I was in Alpine again after thirty-seven years.

The balance between Mike Flynt the coach and Mike Flynt the player was one of the most difficult things to maintain throughout the entire season.

I noticed from the first day of practice that the defense and offense failed to interact with one another to the point where we didn't even know each other's names. I think that's one of the challenges of being a Division III school. Athletic scholarship money isn't available. Players lived in their own places around town rather than together in an athletic dormitory. In my opinion it is impossible to function as a cohesive team if players don't even know the names of their teammates they're depending on to help them win games.

I wanted to rectify that gap. I focused on learning as many of the players' names as I could and said their names whenever possible. At night I studied our game program and made sure I put faces with names, numbers, and positions. The following day at practice I'd yell things like, "Great catch, Corion!" Or "Johnnie, way to cover. Good hit!" Hearing their names made a great difference in the players' performances. It was a natural reaction. They knew that someone was watching them specifically, and that encouraged them to turn up the juice and work even harder.

During our games I would pick out one of our players as they lined up for kick coverage, and I would start hollering encouragement to him. Like, "Kyle, I am watching you. I want to see you make the tackle. Do not get blocked!" Kyle Braddick was a tough kid who played hard, and it was amazing to note the number of times when I singled him out and called his name that he ended up on the tackle. At one game I failed to yell for Kyle; he came up to me on the sideline and said, "Mike, I didn't hear you hollering for me this time. What's up?" I didn't let that happen again the rest of the season!

With every drill the linebackers did as a group, I called out each of their names and always said something positive. I know that enthusiasm is a powerful emotion, and it is also highly contagious. Enthusiasm breeds more enthusiasm and helps players focus. Conversely, complacency and just "going through the motions" creates an acceptance of mediocrity.

Therein lies the truth in the old adage, "You play like you practice."

Because I always watched my teammates, I knew when one of them wasn't at practice. One day Jeremy Cartwright didn't show. I asked the other receivers if they knew where he was, but no one had seen him. I looked for him the next day on campus. I usually saw most of the players at the cafeteria, but still no Jeremy.

I was relieved to see him at practice that afternoon. I approached Jeremy before practice, told him I had missed him the day before, and asked him how he was doing.

He said, "Mike, I'm thinking about quitting."

I said, "Quitting! Why would you do that?"

I was shocked. Jeremy has good size, great speed, and a tremendous work ethic. He said that as he'd walked to class the previous morning, three cow-boys had fallen in step behind him. One of them had said, "If we didn't have basketball and football at Sul Ross, we wouldn't have any niggers here." When they said that, Jeremy stopped and turned around. One of the cowboys spit at his feet, and the three squared up waiting for his response. Jeremy said, "Mike, I might have been able to take a couple of them, but I don't know; I just turned and walked back to my room. I was so depressed I've just stayed in my room for the last couple of days. I think I'm just going to quit and go home."

I was heartbroken for Jeremy as he talked. But I was also furious. Many memories flooded back about how I would have handled something like this in my earlier days at Sul Ross. I told him, "Jeremy, don't you see? What you did was the right thing to do. The decision you made was in the best interest of your teammates. We need you back there running those kickoffs back. We need you out there at wide receiver. There's a no-tolerance policy at this school, and if you had jumped those guys, you would have been gone."

I grabbed him by his shoulders and told him, "Jeremy, you did what I was never able to do! You walked away. I never did, and it cost me everything; I lost it all. For me it was always about immediate gratification and my pride—react and get it done right now. I never thought about consequences, about how other people might be affected by my actions. It was always about me. What you did was amazing, and I'm so proud of you! Who knows, Jeremy, you may go on to become an All-American here at Sul Ross because of that one right decision."

Jeremy reached out and hugged me. He said, "Mike, you are an angel! You are making me feel so good! I can't tell you what talking to you has done for me. I'm not going to quit. I'm going to stay and try to be an All-American."

But then I turned serious and asked, "Jeremy, there is just one thing I need to know. Where can I find those guys?"

Jeremy pulled back, looked at me, and then we both started laughing; it was that genuine kind of laughter that has such a cleansing effect on your soul.

That moment was such an important one for me because it allowed me to catch a glimpse of my younger self and to maybe keep another young man from making a decision he would regret for the rest of his life. I could tell him honestly what a great and unique opportunity he had to play college football and how he should not allow anyone—not ignorant people looking for a fight, or even his own pride—to cause him to give up on his dream in exchange for a few minutes of self-satisfaction.

————————

There were other opportunities disguised in different forms, but I always tried to be sensitive to the needs of my teammates. Sometimes I was restrained.

I asked Coach Wright several times if I could talk to the team as a unit, but he usually denied my request without a reason. I had been fortunate enough to be a part of three very successful Division I football programs and had worked with some quality coaches. I felt that the experiences I had gained from life and the knowledge I had from those winning programs would enable me to help these guys in many ways if I had been allowed to share it.

After the season ended I received a telephone call from one of my teammates, Adam Cuellar. He wanted to check in and catch up. Toward the end of the conversation, he said, "I'm going to be a coach one of these days, and I know there were a lot of times you wanted to talk to us and you weren't allowed to. If I ever see in the teams I coach a player who shows the desire to speak to the team, and I feel like he can make a contribution, I'll never tell him no."

I was grateful Adam was perceptive enough that he understood what I wanted to do and had learned from it. He had noticed the responsibility I felt toward the team, and he had recognized the value in allowing players to be leaders. I think he's going to be a great coach someday, and I am proud to have played alongside him.

Many of my teammates were an inspiration to me as well. They probably don't realize the positive impact they had on me. One such incident was the result of a season-ending injury.

Receiver Jacob Warden suffered a broken leg against East Texas. It was a terrible break, and he was in excruciating pain as the medical team carried him off the field. The next morning, when I went to visit him in the hospital, his leg was in a splint. He was awaiting transport to San Antonio for major surgery to repair the leg and insert a metal pin in the bone. The doctors had told him they weren't sure he'd ever be able to play again.

Obviously, Jacob was feeling pretty down. When I visited him I took him a Powerbase T-shirt as a "get well" gift. A few weeks before the accident, he had visited the Powerbase Web site and jokingly asked me how he could get one of those shirts. I told him I was on pretty good terms with the Powerbase inventor, and I could probably arrange to get him a deal.

I brought the shirt to his room to show him I'd made good on my promise, and then we just sat and talked for a long time. He told me his prognosis from the doctors, and how discouraged it made him feel. I listened to what he had to say, and I could see the fear in his eyes, so I said, "Jacob, it's been my experience that every time you start living in the future, it's usually a bad thing. We've all experienced fear of future problems that never became reality. God doesn't give us the grace to deal with the future; He gives us the grace for today. Today they don't know all the facts, so why don't you start believing right now that you are going to be able to play again?"

I know I'm not a doctor, but I do have pretty good knowledge of the human body. I know after the body heals itself, smart rehabilitation and proper exercise can help to get a limb back into shape. I told Jacob, "You just make up your mind right now that you are going to play. You believe every day as you're going through this healing process that you're going to be able to play until, at some point in time, your body or someone knowledgeable tells you that you can't— and gives you a reason why. But right now, you don't have to accept that. You don't have to tell the doctors you don't accept that, but you know in your heart you don't have to believe them. You believe what you want to believe about the future; you do all you can do to attain that goal and trust God to help you."

When I left, I wasn't sure how he felt about everything we had discussed. But I prayed he wouldn't be discouraged. Intense pain, both emotionally and physically, has a way of redirecting our focus and taking it off our goals. The next day, his girlfriend approached me on campus to tell me that Jacob's spirits were up and that my visit had meant as much to him as had his visit from the college president. She said I had given him hope and reason to believe he would not be beaten by this injury. Jacob's courage and positive attitude in the face of his injury in turn inspired me and helped carry me through the season in dealing with my injuries.

———————

I could never list all the interactions that took place with my teammates— there were just too many—but some were special.

Nathan Graham: All-Conference linebacker, Permian High School graduate. Big Nate, as we called him, reminded me of President Theodore Roosevelt's famous quote: "Speak softly and carry a big stick." That was Nate. Even in practice when we were in shorts and helmets the offensive players made it a point to always know where Nate was and what he was doing. Nobody wanted to get hit by Nate.

Andrew Ross: Another team leader that will really come into his own as a senior. Andrew felt like me being on the team made Sul Ross a closer football team. I know Andrew is one of those returning lettermen that will gladly pick-up the role of team leader and give it his all.

Vinny LaRock: Telling me after one of my talks to the team that he needed to hear those words and how the things I had told him helped him to believe in himself.

Colin White: His faith and obvious love for the Lord were always a blessing to me. He's a very smart and talented quarterback whom Sul Ross is fortunate to have.

Chris Redin: He has the potential to be the best of the best at whatever he does. What a pleasure it was to talk with him as we sat together on road trips.

James McCall: The "Texas Tattoo." Always in the weight room working to improve his game, and always one of those guys I just enjoyed being around.

Eddie Ruiz: Graciously offered me his number 30 when he found out that was the number I wore back in the day. I appreciated the gesture but told him that was the old Mike and I figured number 49 was what I was supposed to have now. He will make me proud of number 30.

Cole Tarleton: One of the first teammates I met when I arrived. He told me I had gone to school with his dad at Sul Ross. Cole was a hitter and just an all-around tough, talented young man.

Curtis Smithson: Another good friend at linebacker. He reminded me a lot of myself when I was young. He told me one of my old teammates, Chris Byerley, coached with his dad.

Ross Guzman: Mentioned to me one day at practice that I used to party with his dad and Dickey Powers down in South Texas. I was hoping they hadn't told him too much about me. Ross is one of those guys you want on your side when things get tough; you can count on him.

Ben Ahrens: Returned from a trip to San Antonio, where he'd had his shoulder scoped for possible surgery. One of the doctors at the clinic asked if Sul Ross was where the "old man" was playing football. Ben quickly responded that the "old man" had a name; it was "Mike." Ben told me he wants to be a coach, and I know he will be a good one.

Bubba Smith: Told me one day at practice that I really needed to push my socks down—said I was out of style. Bubba also told me he loved me and was glad I was on the team. I kept my socks pushed down from that day forward—didn't want to embarrass my teammates.

Shane Robbins: What an inspiration to be around this young man. With so much talent and ability, he is always thinking about getting better and working to make it happen.

Colton Keck: I know he must wake up smiling. Another one of those freshmen who stepped in and played senior-type football.

Andy Mata: Has already put on about fifteen pounds of muscle since the end of the season. Andy has "starter" written all over him.

Baltazar Haro: Will be a player for Sul Ross because he is committed to paying the price it takes to be a winner. He always made me feel like a teammate no matter where we were.

Aubrey Lightheard: An amazing talent to be so young. Aubrey will be an All-Conference player for Sul Ross someday; he's a natural leader who lets his helmet do the talking.

Chase Bowser: I have never seen a big man move as fast as Chase did when he thought T. J. was going to put an earthworm on him. It's no wonder he is such a good offensive lineman—fast and strong.

Marlon Harrison: Called me "Foo Foo" one day in practice. I couldn't believe my ears. It had been over forty-five years since Larry Gatlin had given me the nickname "Foo Foo." Marlon found out about the name from a newspaper article that Larry had written about me in the *Odessa American* newspaper.

Rufino Gutierrez: Another future All-Conference player for Sul Ross. Watching him play, it was hard to believe he was a freshman.

Kyle Braddick: When overhearing some strangers talking about "that old man who is playing football," he jumped in and said, "That old man will kick your butt!"

I knew when I returned to Sul Ross that I would love my teammates. That was just me; I love kids.

And I did love each of these young men.

———————

There was one Sunday early in the season when the coaches left practice and I was able to speak to my teammates. I talked to them about the challenges we faced, not just in football but in life, and how important it was for them to believe in themselves. I told them I wanted to tell them a story I had never heard anyone tell but me. I also told them when I started the story that they were going to think they had already heard it before, but they had not.

I began, "The story is from the Bible; it's about David and Goliath." The players smiled and nodded their heads, but I told them to hang on and let me finish.

"You see, what really happened was the Philistine army was on one hill and the armies of Israel were on another hill facing the Philistines. Each day a guy from the Philistine army named Goliath, who was ten feet tall and weighed about 500 pounds, would walk down into the valley between the hills and challenge the Israelite army to send one man down to fight against him. He did this for forty days, and each day he cursed the Israelites, belittled them, insulted them, and challenged them to send one man down against him.

"Well, then David showed up on the scene and heard this challenge. David was really offended by Goliath's brash behavior and the insults against the armies of God. David had already killed a lion and a bear, so he was thinking, *This dude can't be as strong as a bear or a lion. I can take this guy.* David stepped out in faith, God honored that faith, and David killed Goliath.

"Now here is the part of the story you don't know. Each day for the forty days Goliath made that challenge to the armies of Israel, there were thirty-seven men on that hillside who could have taken Goliath but never stood up. They each had more experience than David. They had more natural ability and more talent and size than David. In every way from a fighting perspective they were far superior to David, but they didn't stand up because they listened to everyone else tell them what their limitations were, what they could and couldn't do. 'No one has ever beaten Goliath. He's ten feet tall and weighs 500 pounds; you can't beat Goliath.' 'You're not big enough!' 'You're not strong enough!' 'You're too slow!'

"One of these men, Adino the Eznite, went on to kill eight hundred men in a day by himself. Another—Abishai, the brother of Joab—killed three hundred in a day. Benaiah, the son of Jehoiada, went down against a lion in a snowy pit and killed him with his bare hands. He also went up against one of Goliath's brothers, took his spear away from him, and killed him with his own spear. These guys became known as David's mighty men, and they were bad to the bone. But they let other people define who they were because they didn't believe in themselves, until David came along and showed them how it was done."

I told my teammates they needed to decide who they were, who and what they wanted to become, and not let anyone tell them differently. I told them they had the ability to hurt themselves more than anyone when they chose to believe the negative things others might say about them. They needed to believe in their abilities, believe in their talents, and believe in their dreams. If they failed, let it be because they failed making a supreme effort to realize their dream, not because they let coaches, parents, peers, or anyone else define who they were and place limitations on them. When you believe in yourself you will step out. Sometimes you will fail, but failure just becomes something that has happened to you, not who you are.

I hate to think about all the people out there who have lived their lives and suppressed their dreams because of limitations someone else placed on them—because someone they loved or trusted just didn't believe in them and placed them on a negative road in life.

———————

There's so much more for student athletes to learn about life from competition than just what appears in the record books. The NCAA broadcasts commercials during major games that are a salute to the vast majority of college athletes who take career paths not involved in playing professional sports. I believe that is an important message.

I knew that most of my teammates would probably go into coaching, and they, in turn, would teach their athletes the things they had learned. I wanted those things to be positive, things that would build men of character and commitment. That's reason enough to not squander the opportunity they had. For not everyone is blessed with a second chance.

Part of my lifelong training philosophy has been to show how something is done rather than just tell someone how to do it. I felt I had an obligation to show my teammates that life is really about the decisions you make, the way you treat the people around you, and the conviction you should have in pursuing the things you feel called to do. They knew I faced real consequences for some spur-of-the-moment stupidity. But they also saw me put that behind me and try again by coming back and making the team thirty-six years later.

I hoped they could see from my actions that the past does not have to define your future; step out in faith and become someone you like and admire. To do that, you have to have good people around you and you have to be a firm source of support for those people who rely on you. You can never quit—first, not on yourself, and then, not on each other. Those are things that have everything to do with winning and nothing to do with the scoreboard. When you focus on those things, the scoreboard has a way of taking care of itself.

One thing Coach Wright and I definitely agreed on was the responsibilities we felt to our respective families. His wife was offered and accepted a position in Wisconsin that was apparently more lucrative than what she had at Sul Ross. Throughout the football season Coach Wright dealt with having to live physically in Alpine where his team was, and emotionally in Wisconsin where his wife and two daughters were—on top of dealing with all of the extra media attention. I know that it had to be a stressful time for him.

At the end of the season when Coach Wright called a team meeting, he asked, "Are there any seniors in here?" He saw the raised hands in the back of the room and thanked the seniors for our leadership. He then made eye contact with me and said, "Mike's here. You guys, it may be several years before you realize how much he's done for your team."

That was the first time all year he had acknowledged me in a positive way in front of my teammates, and I appreciated that.

But then Coach Wright suddenly changed his tone and announced, "I'm not answering any questions. Don't ask me any questions. My resignation from Sul Ross is official as of yesterday. I did this for two reasons: Number one, in the six years I've been here I've coached a lot of you young men who are from single-parent families, and I've seen all the problems that you have had to deal with because of that. Now I'm forcing my children to go through that same thing—to grow up without their dad being there when they need him. So I'm making this decision primarily for personal reasons—to go be with my family. It's the best thing for them and for me.

"The second reason is I graded myself, as I do every year, and I cost you guys the playoffs. We should have been 8-2 with the talent we have in this room, and I blew it. I give myself maybe a D+ to probably a D-. I just didn't do a very good job. My poor coaching performance reinforces my decision to resign. That's all I'm going to say."

Coach Wright turned and walked out the door. That was the last time I saw him.

Dr. Morgan, the university president, stood up and told the players the school had intended to start a search for a new coach, and they wanted to select players from the team to be part of that process. He indicated that he would be letting us know over the next few days who those players would be. There was an awkward silence since no one really knew what to do next.

I raised my hand and asked Dr. Morgan, "Can I talk to my teammates for a minute?"

He said, "Sure."

I stood up and walked to the front, looked out, and saw that the assistant coaches and trainers were still in attendance. I stood there for a minute, and finally Coach Bridges got up and said, "Coaches, all you coaches, come on; get out of here." Coach Bridges understood I didn't want the coaches and support staff in the room.

I wanted to talk to my teammates alone.

I said, "I know a lot of you guys are thinking, *Oh, no, what's going to happen now?* But I can assure you Sul Ross is going to hire a good football coach, and it could well be one of the great assistant coaches we have here now. I think Coach Wright was pretty hard on himself. But I think he probably did the right thing for his family, and that means it will be the right thing for him. You may not realize this for a number of years, because most of you just aren't there yet, but one of these days you will be making decisions based on what's best for your families; just remember, whatever is best for them will probably be best for you."

It was later announced by the administration that our defensive line coach, Wayne Schroeder, would be the next head football coach at Sul Ross State University.

I could not have been more pleased with their decision. He is a man of character and an excellent coach. I know he will do an incredible job in coaching and training my teammates and the new recruits who choose to attend Sul Ross.

And I'm anticipating great things from them in the future.

FIFTEEN   NO MORE REGRETS

In the spring of 2008, Eileen and I had an opportunity to return to Sul Ross with this book's coauthor, Don Yaeger. It was another wonderful opportunity to show off my school, visit Alpine, and catch up with my teammates.

As we walked toward the Sul Ross student center, I saw Jeremy Cartwright and Jamal Johnson standing just outside. A couple of bear hugs later and our reunion was causing a minor commotion. Out of nowhere a dozen other former teammates showed up.

We all congregated around a group of tables in the cafeteria, and the stories started flying. They were nonstop and funny. It wasn't anything like the reunion in San Antonio with my 1970 teammates, but it was just as meaningful.

What was really so special for me was to sit back and listen to my teammates talk with my coauthor about their first impressions of me when I showed up at Sul Ross.

Jeremy smiled and talked about watching me in the locker room on that first day of practice back in August.

"I was wondering why he was putting on pads. *Who is this old guy?* I just kept looking at him. At first it was in a joking way, like, he can't be on the football team. He has to be a coach and is trying on pads for someone else. And then I saw him putting on the helmet and getting ready to go. He was putting it on and making sure it was right. I thought maybe he was going to be part of the team. I asked another coach if he was a player. I asked Coach Bridges, and he said, 'Yeah, he's a linebacker for us.'"

Jeremy continued, "I really got to understand the guy and what he was trying to do, just for the team. He could have done many other things besides be there and struggle with us every day at practice. He was hurt in practice, and he was hurt the whole season, but he was there every day.

"Even I wasn't there every day, but he was."

Then Jamal spoke up—everyone called him J. J. He was one of the smaller guys in the starting lineup, but only because no one has figured out how to weigh a man's heart. J. J. was lightning fast, and many running backs and wide receivers around the conference will attest to his ability to deliver a punishing hit.

J. J. was also an Odessa Permian graduate, so we had clicked from day one. Everyone at the table had a big laugh when J. J. said I was a player—no, make that a starter, a fifty-nine-year-old starter, for the record books—on his NCAA Football '08 video game. "I created the Sul Ross team," he said, "and I've got Mike as one of my starting outside linebackers. He's balling on the NCAA video with about ten tackles a game; he's all right."

J. J. continued, "At our practices, Mike was always interacting with every-body, making sure everyone was in it for the fun of the game. For me, I kind of have a bad attitude. I kind of blow up in situations. It can be something real small, but Mike was always coming to me and grabbing me and pulling me to the side and saying, 'J. J., I see so much potential in you. You are sup-posed to be a leader, and for you to react like you do in certain situations, it's just not good.' He really helped me a lot."

I enjoyed listening to them talk about the things I had told them. I knew they had been listening to me, and that was really gratifying.

Freshman Tim Brooks had told me in the weight room one day that his stepfather was a preacher, and he wanted Tim to hang around me because he had heard I was a good guy. That was a far cry from Randy Wilson's dad, who told him in 1970 that he needed to find a new friend because I wasn't through getting in trouble yet.

Tim said, "I actually saw Mike during the first of August, but I didn't talk to him at first.

"I called my dad and said, 'Dad, there's an old man here playing football with us. His name is Mike Flynt.' And he said, 'I've heard he's a good Christian man.' My stepfather is actually a preacher, so he was like, 'Stay close to him, listen to him, and he'll be an inspiration for the team.' Mike really was too."

Then Justin Hutchinson jumped in and said, "Something would happen and we would all be down and everyone would throw their two cents in, and then Mike would throw in a dollar."

While we were sitting around talking, some of the guys had to leave for class. On their way out they asked me if I wanted to join them for their off-season workout later that afternoon. I told them I wouldn't be late.

We had to rush our schedule for the rest of the afternoon so I could make the workout with my teammates. But as promised, I showed up on time and we went through an intense strength-training circuit. One of the exercises in the circuit was the lift we were doing when I had won the contest back in two-a-days. The players told me they had a new name for that exercise.

It was called the "Mike Flynts."

After our weight workout, Coach Pond sent us down to the practice field and we ran sprints. It was the first time since the latter part of two-a-days in August 2007 that I had been able to run full speed due to the groin strain I battled the entire season. It was a good feeling to be able to run again stride for stride with these guys.

Being back out there with my teammates was wonderful.

In a way, I had come full circle—I had lived with regret for thirty-six years, and then God in His mercy had allowed me to go back, turn it all around, and change the final outcome of that dreaded memory.

I think back on all those years, how I was never able to forgive myself, and that lack of forgiveness only kept the regret alive. Forgiveness—that was the key. Now, with every opportunity I have, I tell people to forgive themselves of regret in their lives, and in those instances where someone else created the regret, forgive them also. Then recycle that negative energy toward a positive goal. It's never too late to tackle your dreams.

As we drove out of Alpine and the beautiful Davis Mountains and headed across the desert to the Midland-Odessa Airport, I was asked why it had been so important to me to work out again with my teammates.

I said I had turned sixty a few weeks earlier, and the window of opportunity for me to be able to do that sort of intense training was fast closing, and I didn't want to look back on the missed chance and say, "I wish, I wish, I wish . . ."

I thought back on a question posed by a reporter after the final game of the 2007 season. He asked if I regretted not getting to play more at linebacker than I had.

I replied, "Absolutely not! For me to say that I regretted anything about this experience would be the most selfish, self-serving position I could ever take."

Finally, for me, there would be no more regrets from my senior year.

AFTERWORD "IS THERE A FOUNTAIN OF YOUTH?"

Experience has taught me that there are two reasons why people don't start or stay committed to a fitness program. Number one, they don't have the time; and number two, it's just not convenient. We live in a fast-paced world, and most days it doesn't feel like we have enough time to catch our breath, let alone work out. I am not exempt. I know the feeling.

Years ago I began to research the benefits of shorter workouts. I wanted to give men, women, and children of all fitness levels a concept they could easily embrace and fit into their busy schedules.

There are many approaches to training and different opinions of what works best. Trainers often preach about being in the "zone" of a particular heart rate for maximum fat-burning benefit. It is generally recommended that you should exercise three times a week for a period of at least twenty minutes to produce an improvement in fitness. Again, how long you exercise depends on your personal goals. But research has shown that there are other effective training techniques that produce better results in less time.

I think everyone agrees that exercise is an important component of general health. But I also think common sense is an important component of general health too. Maybe it's just me, but imagine going to someone who hasn't eaten in three weeks and telling them, "Look, I have a small piece of steak and a glass of milk. But since it's just a few bites of steak and not much milk, it's really not a balanced meal, so I am not going to give it to you." Can you just imagine that starving person's reaction?

I believe those few bites of steak and glass of milk have nutritional value and will benefit that person to some degree. The same can be said of your fitness program. If you only have time to train for five minutes, you will benefit from that workout and be better off from a fitness standpoint than you were before you trained. More and more studies are being conducted on the benefits of shorter, quicker workouts. That's pretty much the way life is. You use a short burst of energy, and then you relax.

When I went back to play football, I had more than one reporter ask me, "Is there a fountain of youth, and if so, what is it?"

My response was, "I believe there is a fountain of youth, and I believe it is strength training."

———————————

Strength training, when done correctly, can be performed at almost any age. The benefits are immediate and lifelong.

Muscles burn calories, muscles determine metabolism, muscles help to pull sugar from the blood for energy. It's muscles as they contract, pulling on the bones, that strengthen the bones and prevent and/or reverse the effects of osteoporosis. Muscles, as they get stronger, relieve the stress placed on the joints and thereby lessen much of the pain caused by arthritis. When we work the voluntary muscles (skeletal muscles under conscious control), it better enables our bodies to work the involuntary muscles (muscles controlled by the brain and nervous system—for example, the pupils of the eye).

After years of experience in the fitness industry, I knew strength training was the answer, not only for me but also for millions of other people. I just needed the incentive to come up with a piece of exercise equipment that filled that huge void.

It happened late in 1998 when I was asked to be a speaker at an in-service physical education teachers' meeting in Nashville, Tennessee. The athletic director at that time, Scott Brunett, had heard about some fitness work I was doing with homeschooled children and asked if I would share some ideas with the Metro area teachers.

As it turned out, many of the teachers present had not been trained at all in physical education. Some were English, history, and science teachers who doubled as physical education teachers for budget reasons. They also talked about increasingly large class sizes, limited budgets for equipment, and a lack of storage space. They asked if I had something to help that was safe, portable, effective, and affordable. Something simple that didn't require a degree in physiology to implement the program.

As I left the conference I simply asked God to take my knowledge of the fitness business, my experience, and my desire to help kids and show me what to do. In a matter of days I had a mental concept of exactly what I wanted to make. Of course, it had to involve strength training.

My experience had taught me that strength training is what works and would also be something all students could participate in. I knew the resistance had to be from tubing because tubing doesn't put stress on the connective tissue in the joints, but I also knew it couldn't be tubing the children stood on, because that never worked. The whole concept started falling into place, and within days I had made my first prototype of the Powerbase.

I went back and met with several teachers from that conference and showed them what I had and asked them if they felt that it would meet their needs and help their students. Eleven of the fifteen teachers whom I met with all asked me the same question: "Can I get one of these for me?" All of a sudden it dawned on me. Maybe I had something that worked for everyone and was worth protecting legally.

I called my good friend and former roommate at Sul Ross, Randy Wilson, in Raleigh, North Carolina, and asked him if I needed to patent my idea. Randy had a company that helped people with patent searches and provided consulting if they wanted to patent and market their idea. I described the Powerbase to Randy. He really didn't want to hurt my feelings, but he said he didn't have a clue what I was talking about. I mailed him a photograph of the Powerbase, and a few days later Randy called and said, "This is brilliant; this is incredible. You came up with this idea?" I said, "Yeah." Randy was impressed, and I was encouraged by his excitement. He conducted a patent search and confirmed I could get a patent on the idea. He also asked if I would be interested in talking to some of his contacts at a couple of infomercial companies. I said sure.

Everyone I met with expressed interest in doing an infomercial with the Powerbase, but I felt American Telecast, based in West Chester, Pennsylvania, was a cut above the other companies. It was a first-class operation and had the reputation of being one of the most successful consumer product and direct-response marketing companies in the world. But I had a minor problem: no one had ever used the Powerbase but me. I visited company officials, who later told me my presentation with the Powerbase had convinced them it was a very good and versatile piece of equipment with a broad demographic base.

American Telecast agreed to produce an infomercial and poured about a million dollars into the project. The company thought the Powerbase had the potential to be the next hula hoop. That was a pretty exciting thing to hear. When the hula hoop was released in 1958 by Wham-O, the company sold more than one hundred million in two years.

Under the terms of our contract, American Telecast had a certain period of time to test the Powerbase and market it before the units went into retail. We actually signed the agreement on September 1, 2001. Of course, ten days later our world changed forever when al-Qaeda terrorists coordinated a series of suicide attacks on the United States.

After things returned to some degree of normalcy, we began to move forward with our project. American Telecast helped me to polish Powerbase into the finished product it is today. With their quality engineers using the finest components, we created a truly amazing piece of equipment.

Weighing less than 4 pounds, the resistance on the Powerbase varies from 5 pounds to over 150 pounds. For resistance, it uses the best quality tubing available, attached to an industrial-grade plastic base in such a way that the tubing can be easily replaced if damaged or worn through use. Each of the tubes has a clip on the end to attach it to various objects to accommodate your workout (padded handles, Velcro straps, and a training bar). The whole package also includes a carrying case and an exercise mat.

When asked about Powerbase, I tell people that if you want to buy a piece of home equipment and you want something portable, ask yourself, "Will this piece of equipment I am considering for purchase give the same workout on the beach as it does in my home?" If the answer is yes, then that equipment is truly portable. The next question is, does it allow you to do all the exercises you want to do? If it doesn't, then you need to find a portable piece of equipment that does.

American Telecast finally shot the infomercial in March 2002, and it aired that June. Since the company had such high expectations for the Powerbase, they signed agreements with Denise Austin, a fitness and exercise expert, and Bill Goldberg, a two-time world heavyweight champion in professional wrestling, to represent the product.

Early testing went quite well. When the contract period expired in 2003, American Telecast asked for an extension, and I agreed. I hoped for even better results the second time around. The company reshot the infomercial, and sales were fine, but the Powerbase didn't generate enough money to pay the overhead of the advanced royalties and the media time. American Telecast wasn't ready to give up. They asked for another extension on our agreement, but after a lot of thought and prayer, I decided to exercise my exit clause in the contract and take the Powerbase back.

The American Telecast experience was wonderful, and everyone involved with their company was first class. But in December 2003, American Telecast and I amicably parted ways, and I began to rethink my marketing approach with the Powerbase. I knew it was time to return to school.

In 2004 I began to introduce the Powerbase into schools. First, I started locally in Williamson County, Tennessee, and then in adjoining states. As of March 2008 the Powerbase and its programs were affiliated with elementary, middle, and high schools in eleven states, including New York, which has some of the most stringent physical education guidelines in the country.

Another special opportunity presented itself in the form of a drug rehabilitation program for young men ages sixteen to twenty-six. They were part of a new concept that was started in Tennessee called Narrow Gate Ministries. The young men who were part of this program lived in tents on one hundred acres at Deer Run Retreat, owned and operated by David and Liz Gibson. The guys worked the land and prepared all their own meals by campfire. I was shocked when we first met—this was truly an outdoor experience.

In addition to studying the Bible and learning about Jesus, they were also rehabilitating from drugs and alcohol abuse. They learned discipline and how to be self-sufficient. The one thing their camp director told me they didn't have was a structured exercise program to help them recover from the ravages of drugs and alcohol on their bodies.

I met with fifteen of these young men one morning and told them how impressed I was by their commitment to improve their lives. I told them if they would give me a 100 percent effort, I would volunteer my time and help them with their fitness. They immediately promised their commitment, and I could see how eager they were to get started.

The camp director purchased fifteen Powerbases, and the following week I trained the "dirty dozen + three" at seven in the morning, four days a week for forty-five minutes per day. It was an amazing experience for them and for me. Most of these guys were in their early twenties, and they worked as hard as anyone I have ever trained. They never missed a workout, and for several of them, these workouts were extremely hard. One of the guys from the Houston area told me he had nightmares of an exercise called "Superman"—you lie on your stomach with resistance on your hands and feet, lifting your legs and arms at the same time like you're flying—but he never missed a workout.

I saw a change in these guys for the better, both physically and mentally. I pushed harder and harder, and they soaked it up. After nearly three months they had reached a point where they no longer needed me, and they led the workouts. I encouraged them, and they in turn inspired me.

All of these young men completed their stay at Narrow Gate. Some have gone on to serve at other drug rehab locations around the country. One night at the movie theater I ran into a few of these young men. They shared with me some of the victories the Lord had given them over their past lives and how they still trained with the Powerbase. Our young people are our nation's greatest resource. Helping them to believe in themselves and improve their lives is the main reason I love coaching.

Ira Green is a man who shares my passion for helping kids. I met him through my dear friend and fellow Powerbase fitness trainer, Jason Daniel. Ira started Camp Timber Creek four years ago to cater to overweight children. The camp is located in the foothills of the Blue Ridge Mountains in North Carolina. For the past three years the children at the camp have used the Powerbase as their primary training source for exercise.

The camp experience lasts for eight weeks, and the children range in ages from eight to eighteen. Ira elected to use the Powerbase because he knew it would be joint friendly and safe for all the campers, and also because of its portability, which allows the children to train in different locations. The campers have lost an average of thirty-plus pounds per child for the past three years. This very positive information is according to statistics collected by East Carolina University and confirmed by officials from Belmont University.

Most of these children leave the camp and continue to train on their own with the Powerbase at their homes. Ira has recently told me that for the first time ever, the camp training will be handled by former campers who have come back to help in appreciation for what the experience has done for them.

All the training I did for Narrow Gate Ministries and providing programs for different children's groups definitely paid off. I was in good shape physically, and this allowed me to step up and embrace what I thought was going to be a "company maker" for Powerbase.

Thanks to a series of phone calls and some amazing connections, I found myself in the "E" ring of the Pentagon in the summer of 2005. I was prepared to make a presentation to an assistant for Lieutenant General H. Steven Blum, head of the U.S. Army and Air Force National Guard. The sergeant major I was scheduled to meet with had forgotten about our appointment and wasn't there. The master sergeant who was to act as his "stand-in" let me know right away in a very cold and authoritative manner that she had other things she needed to be doing. She looked at her wristwatch and said, "I can look at what it is you want to show the sergeant major. You've got fifteen minutes, starting now."

I explained to her that the piece of equipment I had is called the Powerbase and is portable. I told her it will fit in a soldier's rucksack, and every soldier can carry one. They can train on their own, or they can train together as a unit. They never have to miss a workout. As I spoke, I took the Powerbase out of the carrying case and explained, "Okay, here's what you do." And I started the workout. As she watched me her face was relaxed, her eyes focused. I thought, *Hey, this is a workout person. She gets this.* And then she started to ask questions. I invited her to try the exercises, and the next thing I knew, I looked at my watch and it had already been forty-five minutes.

The master sergeant then asked her counterpart from the air force to step inside the room. Fifteen minutes later, another sergeant arrived. She was in charge of training for all employees at the United States Army Combat Readiness/Safety Center in Arlington, Virginia. The three of them talked together and said, "Okay, we've got to do some testing on this. Can you come back?"

I told her, "Sure. What do you want me to do?" She said her staff would select about fifty of their trainers in the Washington, D.C., area. These fifty people are responsible for training the U.S. Army and Air Force National Guard, and they wanted me to put them through a workout on the Powerbase.

"Can you do that?" she asked.

I told her, "Yes, I can. That's a piece of cake."

Approximately two weeks later I drove back to Arlington with another trainer, Jason Daniel, and other support people who had been responsible for getting me in the door at the Pentagon. Jason is the very best at what he does; I couldn't run Powerbase without him.

Fifty trainers waited on us, and everyone was dressed in their workout gear. We handed each one of them a Powerbase, and I explained to them, "I am going to take you through this workout, and we're going to get it done in thirty minutes max. Then I am going to show you some exercises you can do individually and as a team. All right, here we go."

The command sergeant major—the gentleman who had missed our interview and was the right-hand man for General Blum—went through the entire workout. He was nearly my age and was in great shape. The trainers did well for most of the workout. Some were in better condition than others, which became obvious as we neared the end of our workout. Overall, as a group they did an outstanding job.

At the end I said, "Okay, now I am going to show you a few exercises you can do individually, and then I'm going to show you some fun stuff you can do with your units as a group." We went through each exercise; they picked up on them quickly, and from the looks on their faces, I knew they enjoyed the workout.

Each trainer who participated that day was required to submit an evaluation review of the workout and turn it in before leaving the Readiness Center. The sergeant who scheduled the training session called me a few days later and told me it was the first time they had received a 100 percent "Hoo-ahh" on any fitness equipment evaluation. They loved the Powerbase and asked if I could return and train their general population of seven hundred persons in the Readiness Center.

In my excitement, I committed, "Yes, I can do that."

Jason, his wife, Melissa, who also was a fitness trainer, and I geared up and for the next nine weeks trained the National Guard at the Arlington Readiness Center. I even made a special DVD workout for General Blum and was told by his personal assistant, Master Sergeant George Blalack, that the general thought the Powerbase was a great workout and did it faithfully.

One of the more memorable experiences during this training time came when we went outside and utilized the half-mile track adjacent to the center. We had some Special Forces members who trained with us as well as the regular Guard. The side of the center that overlooked the track is all glass, so everyone on that side of the building watched the fun.

At every eighth-mile mark on the track was an asphalt square that served as an exercise station. We positioned Powerbase units at each station with signs that indicated the exercises to be performed there: for example, "Squats," "Shoulder Press," or "Triceps Extensions and Biceps Curls." The course was designed to provide a complete body workout, in both strength and endurance.

We started with several men and/or women at each station. One of my trainers stood in the middle of the track with a timer and a whistle. The program was designed to be high intensity with very little rest between exercises. The trainer blew the whistle, and everyone started strength training at their station. After several seconds the trainer blew the whistle and everyone sprinted in unison, counter-clockwise, to the next station and waited for the command to exercise. This was repeated until everyone had completed the circuit.

We really pushed those people. Most of them were in great shape, but for some of them the demands of the high-intensity training were too great a challenge and they dropped out. But these same soldiers later told us they maxed out their personal training tests because of their increased strength and endurance generated by the training.

The Guard purchased units for the Arlington soldiers and then wanted us to travel to Little Rock, Arkansas, to the boot camp center for the National Guard, and train their people. They were excited about the Powerbase, and there was talk of making it standard issue for all the National Guard.

I explained to them that due to the time and financial commitment required for an undertaking of that magnitude, I was not in a position to go forward without a purchase order. They told me they completely understood my position.

The purchase of Powerbases for the Readiness Center in Virginia was not a problem, because it was termed as "fitness equipment" for the center. But to get a purchase order from the National Guard for the significant number of

Powerbases that would be needed for Little Rock was another matter entirely.

The very long and slow legal process to get that accomplished ensued as the personnel in charge of the training sought to gain "authorization" to purchase Powerbases. I know how enthused the people I personally dealt with were about making the Powerbase available to all our men and women in the military. But with conflicts around the world and the complexity of an undertaking on that scale, it may take quite awhile to get that request pushed through.

I am both proud and grateful that we were able to help our military, even in a limited capacity; it was a very rewarding experience.

It has been over eight years since I invented the Powerbase. I have had some disappointments, but more victories, and nothing has ever dampened my enthusiasm for this equipment.

My philosophical approach to fitness as a coach, trainer, and teacher hasn't changed. I never ask anyone to do something that I am not willing to do myself. I learned many years ago that what I do—or don't do, as the case may be—speaks far louder than what I say.

Over the past four years the Powerbase has provided me with many opportunities to help people, and I have been able to stay in shape in the bargain. My main focus initially with the Powerbase was children and folks like me, the baby boomers.

I would love for good health to be a motivational tool for people of all ages. I turned sixty on January 23, 2008, and I feel good all the time. I know I am blessed and I am grateful, but I also train hard and work at staying in shape. That's a message I want to share with as many people as I can.

Had I not been training and helping these different groups over the past seven years, there is no way that at age fifty-nine I could have taken advantage of the opportunity when Sul Ross coach Steve Wright looked at me and said, "I'm going to give you a chance to make this team."

ACKNOWLEDGMENTS

Of all the wonderful blessings in my life, none is greater than the incredible family with which God has blessed me. My wife and children mean everything to me. They have always been the motivation for everything meaningful I attempt in my life and my greatest source of support—even before I suited up in a football uniform again.

After Eileen and I married, we remained in Arlington before I tried my hand at the insurance business, and my new job took us to Lubbock. It was there that we celebrated the birth of our first child in 1974, our daughter Delanie. Our parents were almost as excited as we were; she was the first grandbaby on Eileen's side and the second on my side, sharing the same birthday, May 2, as her only cousin at that time, Trisha.

Delanie entered the world kicking and screaming, and this precious blessing forever changed our lives. I had always loved the name Delanie (from the 1970s singing group Bonnie and Delaney), and it just "fit" for this beautiful, perfect little girl who so captivated our hearts and charmed everyone.

By the time Lanie (the nickname Eileen's mother gave her) was two, I was taking her to the gym with me for workouts. She walked at nine months and talked before she was one year old. Lanie never met a stranger and would walk right up to anyone, say "hi," and brag about being able to "button and zip and tie." She was very quick to show off the pretty ruffles on her panties (I made sure she outgrew that one early!), and her constant command was, "Look at me! Look at me!"

Of our three children, Delanie is definitely the most like me. A "daddy's girl" from day one, she always thought everything I did was cool. She started in gymnastics at age four—an inevitable move given the amount of time she had spent with me at the gym. Fearless and amazingly strong, she kept us constantly on our toes, ever ready to catch her as she climbed everything she possibly could. She was the epitome of trust. I took her to the park, let her climb on a ten-foot slide platform, and asked her to jump to me. She never hesitated and never doubted that I would catch her.

Delanie loved gymnastics and stayed with it during all of her school years. She was an accomplished gymnast and a cheerleader in middle and high school. She was also incredibly fast and one of the best sprinters on the track team. She helped her school win the district title in 1988. After she graduated from high school, Delanie attended Middle Tennessee State University in Murfreesboro, where she began studies toward a degree in interior design and became a member of Chi Omega.

I was coaching at Texas A&M when Micah was born in 1980. Micah also shared a cousin's birthday—he and my sister's daughter, Tamara, were both born on June 6. Unlike in 1974 when Delanie was born, I was allowed in the delivery room with Eileen. The whole experience was amazing, and it's hard to describe the feelings I had when the doctor told us the baby was a boy. At nine pounds, seven ounces, he was already quite handsome.

My mother and Eileen's mother were both at the hospital, and they shared in the excitement. I couldn't wait to call my dad and Eileen's dad and tell them the news. Micah was the only boy born on either side of the family. Eight girls and one boy, and he has enjoyed all of the attention from his sisters and cousins from day one.

We learned at a very early age that Micah had an amazing memory. He loved dinosaurs, so Eileen purchased him a dinosaur book. It was an advanced book that involved scientific details and several extremely long words. We would read that book to him before bedtime at night as he sat and listened with incredible concentration.

One day I heard him in his room as he "read" every page of the book, word for word. He was only five, and I was absolutely amazed. How could a child have that sharp of a memory? It also reminded me that I constantly needed to watch what I said and did around him, because he absorbed and retained everything he took in. We later had more than one teacher tell us he had a photographic memory.

Just like my dad and I had done, Micah and I boxed together for the first time when he was about four. I taught him how to guard himself against punches and how to punch and throw combinations. The main difference between my lessons with Micah and my dad's lessons with me was that I never once hit my son.

We enjoyed boxing for years, and even after we quit, we would "shadow-box" against each other. I let Micah hit me until he was about twelve, but after that he had just gotten too strong. I had started him in strength training too. Micah was a big kid and a very nice-looking young man. We laughed about the fact that from age ten to fifteen his shoe size was the same as his age. He ended up being six foot three and around 220 pounds. Ever since he was a teenager, I've told Micah that he was my hero. As I watched him grow and observed the way he handled himself, I couldn't help but admire him and the things he chose to do or not do. He was always wise beyond his years.

Our youngest daughter, Lillian Marie, was born here in Franklin in 1988, and we named her after two very special people in our lives: our moms.

This precious baby girl was the focus in all our lives. With an older brother and sister always doting on her, she was able to learn from each of them, and she assumed all the best qualities from both of her siblings.

Lily never saw herself as being younger and always wanted to do everything her brother and sister did. With her "can do" spirit, beauty, athleticism, and intelligence, she has always been a charmer. Like her sister before her, she is a "daddy's girl" and I cherish the memories of all the hours we shared when she was a little girl, playing together with dolls and living on a make-believe farm.

Blessed with her mother's speed and amazing hand-eye coordination, she was a natural in softball and track. She could hit the ball a mile, and it was such a treat to watch her pull away from the competition as she ran sprints in track.

Always a perfectionist, Lily was a teacher's dream, and it was so nice to hear her teachers from kindergarten through high school talk about what a special person and student Lily was. We knew that already, but it was good to hear.

God performed an amazing miracle in Lily's life when she was very young and healed her of a platelet disorder that kept us on our knees for almost five years. We have always called her our "miracle child."

———————

Delanie the woman is true to Lanie the excited little girl. She enjoys decorating and all things in the art world. She is also an aspiring actress. She has had a variety of acting jobs in college, music videos, television, and Internet commercials. She married a wonderful young man, Ben Swanson, an accountant from Nashville. Lanie has never given up on her dream to someday make it in the movies. We keep telling her that she has been performing since day one, and it is just a matter of time before the right part and the right connections come along to give her that big break. In the meantime, she is a fantastic mother to our precious two-year-old grandson, Collin Michael. With blond hair and beautiful blue eyes, he is, of course, the most handsome little guy in the world, and the whole family absolutely adores him.

Micah graduated from high school with honors and then went on to complete his undergraduate studies and a master's degree in nutrition sciences from the University of Tennessee, Knoxville. He is a registered dietician and not only works full-time for Summit Medical but also teaches a nutrition science course at UT. Micah married his high school sweetheart, our beautiful daughter-in-law Jennifer, who will be a certified family nurse practitioner when she graduates from UT.

Growing up, Micah was very athletic, playing baseball, football, and soccer. He was musically talented and played the piano as well. But he enjoyed sports much more, both as a spectator and as a participant. While at UT, one of his professors suggested that he try a marathon, so he trained and ran in the Knoxville City Marathon, which qualified him for the prestigious Boston Marathon. I've never even come close to running twenty-six miles at one time.

Our Lily was extremely active throughout school as part of the student council, Honor Society, and homecoming court. Her senior year she achieved her Gold Award in Girl Scouts, having stayed with the same troop and group of girls since second grade. She played the piano, modeled, and also was very athletic, participating in soccer, softball, track, and gymnastics. She was on the middle school dance team and was a cheerleader in high school. After high school she enrolled at the University of Tennessee in Knoxville on a full academic scholarship. We have always called her our "Sunshine" because of her consistent happy attitude, her beautiful smile, and her love for our family.

The most amazing thing about my family is the fact that even before I hit the gridiron again, they were my biggest fans and my loudest cheerleaders. In everything I have attempted, they have been there for me. All three of them called almost daily when we were in Alpine, just to check on Eileen and me and offer words of encouragement and support. I still have a message from Delanie on my cell phone that she left me not long after I made the team, telling me how proud she is of me. I have kept notes from Lily and Micah saying the same. I certainly have more than I ever dreamed of or deserve in a family.

———————

Webster's Dictionary describes *family circle* as "the close members of a family and intimate friends." As well as my immediate family, I am blessed to have my extended family as well.

Throughout our thirty-five years of marriage, my family and Eileen's have been supporting me in good times and bad. My mother; my sisters, Gwen and Pam; Pam's husband, Charlie; along with my nieces, Carla, Tamara, and Trisha; and two of their husbands, Mitchell and Paul, traveled many miles by plane and car to attend several of my games during my final season of football.

Work kept my other brother-in-law, Joe, and Carla's husband, Chad, from coming. My niece, Tamara, had gray T-shirts printed to resemble game jerseys for all the family to wear to the games. In big red letters they read "# 49" on the front, and "Flynt # 49" on the back. It was so cool to look up in the stands and see those shirts.

I was fortunate to have my two sisters. My older sister, Gwen, has always loved me, and no matter what I needed, she has never told me no. My younger sister, Pam, has always placed me on a hero's pedestal, and no matter how much trouble I got into (and I got into a lot), she always proudly stated, "That's my brother!" and continued to love me as only a little sister can.

Eileen's sweet eighty-nine-year-old mother, Eileen's sister Becky and her husband, Everett, and our niece Kim and her husband, Kevin, all drove from Oklahoma to attend the game in Brownwood against Howard Payne. Counting the family from Oklahoma, Texas, and Tennessee, we had nineteen family members in the stands sporting their "Flynt" shirts. Our other nieces and their husbands, Amber and Oz, and Robyn and Bernd, were unable to attend any of the games but always called and offered their support.

Our church family at the People's Church in Franklin, Tennessee, along with our pastor, Rick White, has been praying for us for the past twenty-three years. We are so grateful for their love and friendship.

My teammates and coaches from that Permian High state championship team in 1965 will always be a part of my family. They were among the first people I notified that I intended to return to Sul Ross to try and make the team. Their support was immediate and complete. They all believed in me and encouraged me to go forward. Throughout the season they called and sent e-mails, and many of them came to games to offer their support and encouragement.

My Sul Ross teammates from 1969 and 1970—the guys I let down who so graciously forgave me and held me blameless in their eyes—are special as well. They showed up at the games in force, in support of not only me but the whole Sul Ross team. The experience for them has renewed their love of our school, and they have donated thousands of dollars to help support the athletic programs at Sul Ross. I know that is only the beginning.

The former students from Sul Ross who showed in the thousands and called themselves the "Baby Boomers" not only gave me verbal support but sent e-mails and letters. They made donations to Sul Ross on my behalf and accepted, sent cards and gifts to, and cared for Eileen like she was one of their own. I can never thank them enough. While there are too many to name, I must acknowledge Corra Ward, Gaby Hill, Patti Payton Miles, Toyah Taylor, Gerry Trull and Linda Wilson. There are others I have talked about previously, and many more who made up this wonderful family. The things they did behind the scenes were all a huge part of this experience, and Eileen and I are so grateful for them. Go Lobos!

Many thanks to Jaime Aron for the outstanding job he did in covering my story for the Associated Press throughout the season. He was the first reporter I agreed to interview with and the first to release my story. Not only is he a talented and professional man of character, but we have become good friends through the experience.

Last but not least, I want to express my gratitude to Dr. Tschauner, who graciously worked me in at his chiropractic clinic when I was in Odessa. His professional help played a big part in my successful recovery from two bulged discs.

I look forward to cultivating these renewed friendships and new friendships over the coming years. The year 2007 was special in many ways, but none more than the closeness I shared with my family.

I love them all.